APPLE WATCH SERIES 7 USER GUIDE

A Complete User Manual with Step By Step Instruction For Beginners And Seniors To Learn How To Use The New Apple Watch Series 7 Like A Pro With WatchOS Tips & Tricks

BY

HERBERT A. CLARK

Copyright © 2021 HERBERT A. CLARK

All rights reserved. No part of this book shall be reproduced, stored in a retrieval system, or transmitted by any means, electronic, mechanical, photocopying, recording, or otherwise, without written permission from the publisher. Although every precaution has been taken in the preparation of this book, the publisher and author assume no responsibility for errors or omissions. Nor is any liability assumed for damages resulting from the use of the information contained herein.

LEGAL NOTICE:

This book is copyright protected and is only for personal use. This book should not be amended or distributed, sold, quote, or paraphrased without the consent of the author or publisher.

Table of Contents

INTRODUCTION 1
FEATURES OF APPLE WATCH SERIES 7 2
   Design 2
   Colours & materials 3
   Durability 5
   Always-On screen 7
   Health Features 8
   Battery & Charging 8
   Storage space 9
   WatchOS 8 9
SETUP YOUR APPLE WATCH 10
SETUP A FAMILY MEMBER'S WATCH 18
   Manage a family's members watch 21
BASICS 22
   Apple Watch Series 7 22
   Apple Watch gestures 23
   Watch app 24
   Charge your Apple Watch 26
      Setup the charger 26
      Start charging your Watch 26
   Save power when your watch battery is low 29

How to open applications on your watch 30
Always On feature 31
Wake your Watch display 32
Go back to the clock face 33
Wake up to your last activity 33
Keep the Apple Watch screen on longer 34
Select a language or region 34
Change Wrist or digital Crown orientation 35
Calculate a tip & split the check 37
Set a timer 37
Get directions on your watch 38
Adjust the text size 39
Restart your watch 40
Forces restart your watch 40
Erase your watch & settings 40
Backup your watch 41
Update the software of your watch 42

CUSTOMIZE YOUR WATCH 43
Display your applications in a list or on a grid ... 43
Launch applications from the Home Screen 44
Re-arrange your applications in grid format 46

Remove an application from your Watch...........48
Make changes to the application settings...........49
See the storage space an application is using.....49
Download an Application Store on your Watch.50
Install applications you already have on your iPhone... 51
Tell time on your Watch 51
Open or close the Control Center 52
Change the Control Centre arrangement 54
Remove things from the control centre...............54
Theater mode 55
Find your iPhone...56
Adjust the brightness & text on your Watch 57
Adjust your watch volume..................................58
Adjust the haptic strength of your Watch 58
Activate or Deactivate Digital Crown haptics.....60
Reply to a message when it arrives..................... 61
Manage your Apple ID settings with your Watch 62
Create an emergency Medical ID 63
Connect your Watch to Wi-Fi.............................64

Connect your Watch to headphones or Bluetooth speakers 65

Monitor the volume of your headphone.............66

Handoff Tasks from your watch 67

Use your Apple Watch to unlock your Mac 69

Unlock your iPhone with your Watch 71

Turn cellular on or off 73

Set an alarm on your watch 74

HOW TO CHANGE THE APPLE WATCH BAND . 76

Solo Loop...78

Milanese Loop 79

Remove the Link Bracelet 79

APPLE WATCH FACES 82

Customize your watch face from your iPhone....82

Customize the watch face from your Watch.......84

Set your watch ahead...89

Share and receive a Watch face 89

FOCUS 92

Activate or deactivate a Focus 92

Create your Focus..94

Create a Focus schedule 94

Deactivate or delete a Focus schedule................96

WORKOUT APP 98
  Start a workout 98
  Create a target speed for outdoor run exercises
  100
  Combine many activities in a single exercise ... 101
  Finish, pause, or lock your workout 102
  Monitor your progress 103
  Get reminders to start working out 104
  Get reminders to finish your workout 105
  Activate DND 106
  Save power while working 106
  Use gym equipment with your Watch 107
  Start a swimming workout 109
  Update your weight & height 109
  Change the measurement units 110
  Automatically pause running and cycling workout
  111
FALL DETECTION 112
  Activate or deactivate fall detection 115
  Setup your Medical ID and add emergency contacts 117
HANDWASHING FEATURE 119

Activate hand washing 119

Get hand washing notifications 121

ACTIVITY APP 123

Check your progress 124

Check your weekly summary 125

Change your goals 126

View your activity history 126

View your trends 127

View your awards 128

Control activity reminders 129

Suspend daily coaching 131

Share your activity 131

View the progress of your friends 132

Compete with your friends 133

Adjust the friend settings 134

MEASURE BLOOD OXYGEN LEVEL WITH YOUR WATCH 136

Setup Blood Oxygen 136

Deactivate background measurement in theater & sleep mode 137

Measure the oxygen level of your blood 137

See the history of your blood oxygen measurements 139
COMPASS 140
   View your bearings, coordinates, incline, & elevation 140
   Add the elevation complication to your watch face 141
SCHOOLTIME 143
   Setup SchoolTime... 143
   Leave School-Time 144
   See when School Time was unlocked 145
CYCLE TRACKING 146
   Setup Cycle Tracking 146
   How to track your cycle 147
   Add cycle factors.. 148
   What the colours mean 150
   Log your cycle on your watch 151
   How to check the date for your next & last period 152
   How to set fertility & period tracking notifications & prediction info 152
   How prediction is calculated 154
   How to hide the cycle tracking application 154

PHONE & CONTACT APP 156
   View contacts on your watch 156
   Communicate with contacts 157
   Create a contact 158
   Share, edit, or delete contacts 159
   Make a call 159
   Enter a phone number 159
   View call details 160
   Answer a call 160
   While on a call 162
   Listen to voicemail 163
ECG 164
   How to use the ECG application 164
   Install & setup the ECG application 164
   Perform an ECG 166
   How to read the results 169
   Inconclusive 170
   View & share information about your health 171
   How to get the best results 172
HEART RATE APP 173
   View your heart rate 173

Check your heart rate while working out 174
See your heart rate data chart 175
Get low or high heart rate notifications 175
Get irregular heart rhythm alerts 176

MAIL 177
Select which mail-box appears on your Watch . 177
Read the emails in the mail application 178
Switch to your iPhone 178
Create a message 180
Compose a message 180

MEMOJI 183
Create Memoji 183
Edit a Memoji, Create a Memoji watch face, and more 184

MINDFULNESS 186
Start a meditation or breathing session 186
Set the duration of a session 187
Adjust the mindfulness settings 188
Make use of the Breath watch face 189
Begin a guided meditation 190
View Meditations you have completed 190

NOISE 192

Setup the Noise application..................................193

Receive noise alerts 193

Deactivate noise measuring 193

See the details of a noise notification 193

Checkout your exposure to the ambient sound levels over time..194

CONTROL YOUR APPLE TV WITH YOUR WATCH 195

Connect your Watch to Apple TV 195

Control your Apple Tv with your watch 196

Disconnect & remove the Apple TV...................197

SLEEP APP 198

Setup Sleep on your watch 199

Turn off or edit your next wakeup alarm 199

Add or change a sleep schedule.........................200

Adjust sleep options 201

Check out your recent sleep history 203

Check your breathing rate 203

VOICE MEMOS APP... 204

Record a voice memo 204

Play a voice memo 205

WALKIE-TALKIE 206

Add your friends to the Walkie-Talkie application 206

How to accept Walkie-Talkie invitations 208

Start a Walkie-Talkie conversation 209

Talk over Walkie-Talkie 209

Activate or deactivate Walkie Talkie 210

If you cannot find the Walkie-Talkie application 211

APPLE PAY 212

Add a card to your watch................................... 212

Pick your default card... 213

Change a card's order 213

Remove a card 213

Find a card's Device Account Number 214

Change your transaction details........................ 215

If the Apple Watch is lost or stolen 215

Pay for purchase in a store 215

Buy things in an application.............................. 216

INTRODUCTION

The Apple Watch Series 7, released in September 2021, is the current version of the Apple Watch. The Apple Watch Series 7 introduces some new features which include a larger display, faster charging, & improved durability.

The Apple Watch Series 7 is available in new 41 mm & 45 mm size options, 1mm larger than the previous 40 mm & 44 mm size options. The Apple Watch Series 7 price starts at $ 399 for the 41 mm model. The larger 45 mm model's price begins at $ 429. For cellular compatibility, which allows your watch to optionally work untethered from your Phone, You would spend $ 499 for the 41 mm or $ 529 for the 45 mm size.

FEATURES OF APPLE WATCH SERIES 7

Design

The design of the Watch Series 7 is based on the round, square shape of the foregoing generation, but now it has 41 mm & 45 mm bezel sizes to suit the needs & size of users. The design of the Apple Watch Series 7 has been polished-up with softer & more rounded edges. Although the casings are now a bit larger, they still work with bands of the foregoing generations.

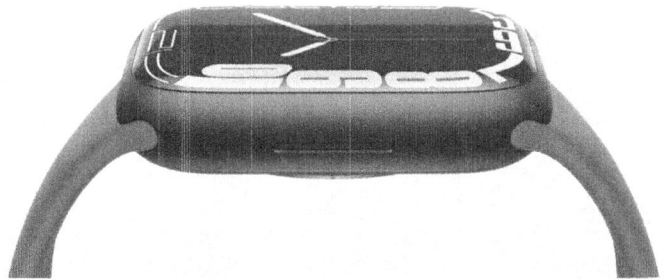

All Apple Watch Series 7 models have ceramic and crystal backs with 4 LED clusters & 4 photodiodes to make it easier for health-monitoring features to function.

There's a Digital Crown on the watch's side which can be used for navigation & scrolling, there's also a Side button that can be used to confirm Apple Pay purchases, access emergency services, etc.

The Digital Crown has haptic feed-back that gives a clear feel when you scroll through lists & control various aspects of your watch, the Digital Crown also serves as a key for the ECG application because it has an inbuilt electrode that works in tandem with the back sensors.

Colours & materials

The Apple Watch Series 7 comes in 3 different materials: titanium, stainless steel, & aluminum. The aluminum model is the cheapest while the titanium model is the most expensive.

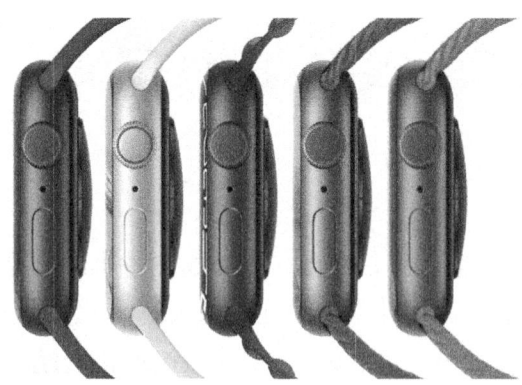

Apple has released 4 new aluminum colours this year: Blue, Green, Starlight, & Midnight. These are supplemented with the PRODUCT RED shade from the 6th series. The stainless steel Apple Watch model comes in graphite, gold, & silver. The Titanium model comes in a natural colour (a silver gray) and Space Black.

In terms of weight, the Apple Watch Series 7 models weigh 10% heavier than the Series 6. The weight of each model is listed below:

41 mm

❖ Titanium: 37.0g
❖ Stainless steel: 42.3g
❖ Aluminum: 32.0g

45mm

- ❖ Titanium: 45.1g
- ❖ Stainless steel: 51.5g
- ❖ Aluminum: 38.8g

Durability

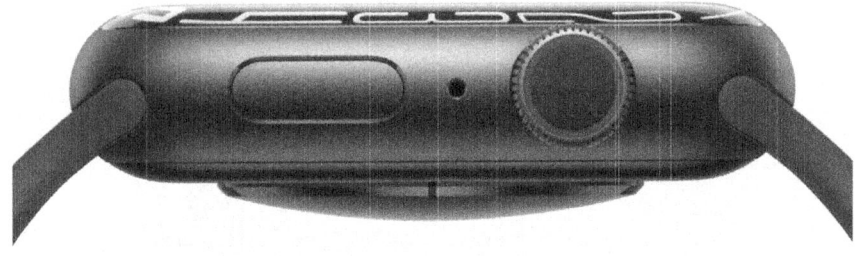

The Series 7 has a stronger, redesigned crystal component with a more reliable geometry. The watch is about 50% thicker than the foregoing model and more resistant to cracking.

The aluminum model has an Ion-X glass that protects the screen, while the stainless steel & titanium models feature a sapphire crystal glass. Sapphire crystal glass provides better resistance than X-Ion glass, as it is a more complex material, which means that models with sapphire crystal are more resistant to everyday wear & scratching.

The Series 7 has an IP6X dustproof rating, which makes it more durable for environments like the desert or the beach.

The Series 7 has a WR50 waterproof rating, which means you can use the watch in water as deep as 50m due to seals & glue. The speaker is the only inlet and is designed to remove water with sound vibrations.

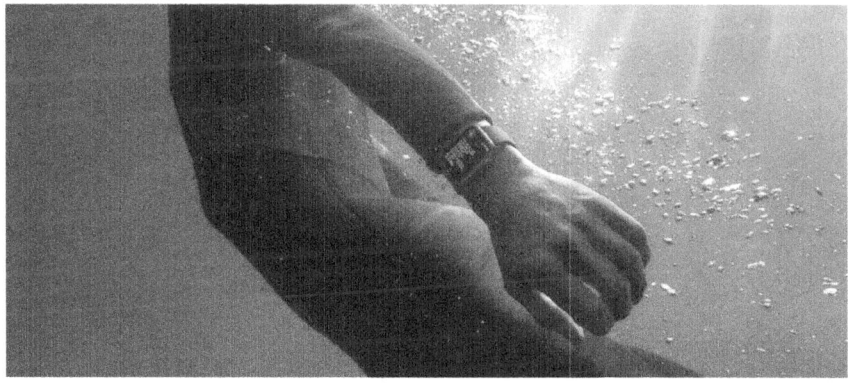

Because it counts for 50m of immersion, you can use the Series 7 to swim in a pool or the ocean. It can only be used for shallow-water activities and cannot be used for showering, waterskiing, scuba diving, or other high-speed water activities, or deep submersion.

Your watch warranty doesn't cover water damages, so it's best to be careful when you expose the watch to water.

Always-On screen

The Series 7 has a bigger screen area. This was achievable by decreasing the borders to only 1.7mm, which is 40 % smaller than the border of the Series 6. The new screen bends slightly around the glass top edges.

The Apple Watch Series 7's screen (right) compared to the Apple Watch Series 6 (center) and the Series 3 (left)

The Apple Watch Series 7 has an OLED ultra low power temperature poly-silicon & oxide screen that allows the Always-On feature to function.

The screen dims when your wrist is down to save battery life. Touching the face of the watch or raising your hand will bring the screen back to full brightness.

Health Features

The Apple Watch Series 7 offers health-tracking features just like the Series 6. A 2nd-gen optical heart-rate sensor measures metrics such as a very high heart rate, resting heart rate, & calorie burn. You can use the electrical heart-rate sensor to take electrocardiograms, while the LEDs & infrared light allow users to track blood oxygen. An inbuilt gyroscope & accelerometer allow for other important health-related features like Fall detection to function properly.

The Apple Watch can detect irregular, high, & low heart rates. The device can also track health issues such as atrial fibrillation, and the device would send alerts when it detects anomalies.

Battery & Charging

The Watch Series 7 provides an "all-day" 18-hour battery life from a single charge. The 45 mm Apple Watch Series 7 is said to have a 1.189Wh (309mAh) battery, which is about 1.6% bigger than that of the Series 6, while the 41 mm model has a 1.094Wh battery inside.

The Apple Watch can charge up to 33% faster than the Apple Watch Series 6 because of the new charging design and Apple's Magnetic Fast Charger USB-C Cable and 18W adapter. This implies that 8 minutes of charging time provides about 8 hours of sleep monitoring.

Storage space

Like the Series 6, the Apple Watch Series 7 model has 32 GB of storage for applications, podcasts, music, etc.

WatchOS 8

WatchOS 8 is the operating system installed in the Apple Watch Series 7. WatchOS 8 provides new features that can help users stay active, healthy, & connected with family & friends.

SETUP YOUR APPLE WATCH

To setup & make use of your Smart watch, you need an iPhone that has the latest version of iOS installed inside. You should also ensure that your iPhone is Bluetooth enabled and connected to Wi-Fi or a mobile network.

Switch on your Watch and wear it on your wrist

To switch on your smart watch, long-press the side button till the Apple icon shows on the screen. This may take a few minutes.

Bring your watch near your iPhone

Wait for the "**Use iPhone to setup this Apple Watch**" alert to show on your Phone, and touch the **Continue** button. If this message does not show up on your iPhone's screen, just launch the Watch application on your iPhone, touch **All Watches**, touch **Pair New Watch**.

If this is your watch, touch **Setup for Myself.** Or, touch **Setup for a Family Member.**

Ensure that your Watch & your Phone are close to each other till you finish the setup process.

Keep your Phone over the animation

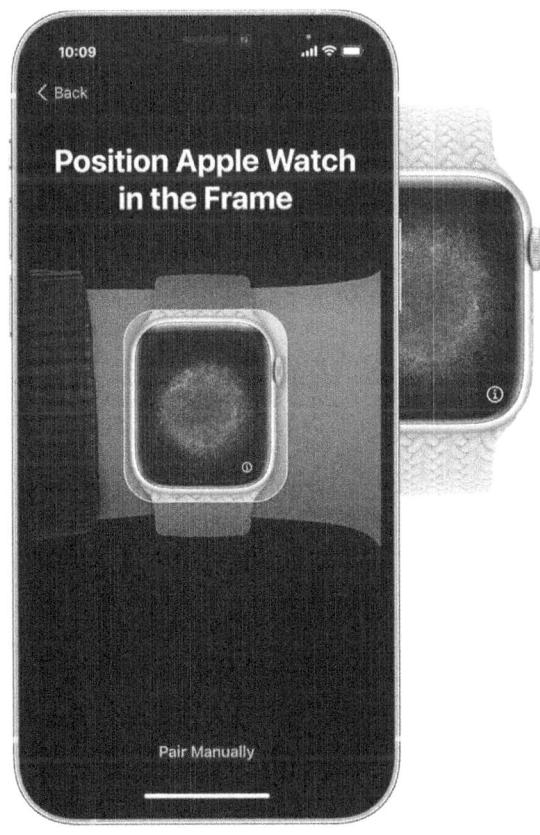

Position your iPhone in a way that the watch face can be seen on the view finder. Wait for an alert that the Apple Watch is paired.

If you cannot utilize your iPhone's camera, or if you did not see the pairing message, touch **Pair Apple Watch Manually**, and adhere to the guidelines on your display.

Set up as new or Restore from backup

If this is your first Apple Watch, click on **Set up as a New Apple Watch**. Or, touch the **Restore from Backup** button.

Read and Agree to the terms & conditions by tapping on the Agree button.

Log in with your Apple ID

If prompt, insert your Apple ID login code. If your Apple ID is not requested, you can login later from the Apple Watch application: Touch General> Apple ID, then log in.

If Find My is not setup on your iPhone, you will be told to enable Activation Lock. If you see the Activation Lock screen, your Watch is already linked with your Apple ID. You must enter the Apple ID's e-mail & password to continue setup.

Select your settings

The Apple Watch would show you the settings it shares with your Phone. If you enable features like Location Services, Find My, Diagnostics, & WiFi Calling for your Phone, these settings will automatically activate on your Apple Watch.

After that, you can decide to utilize other settings, like Siri & Route Tracking. If you have not already setup Siri on your Phone, it will activate after you select this option. You can also pick the text size for your smart watch.

Generate a login code

You can skip creating a login code, but you need one to make use of Apple Pay and some other features.

Touch **Add Long Pass-code** or **Create a Pass code** on your Phone, go to your Apple Watch to enter your new code. Touch Don't Add Passcode to skip this step.

Select Features & Applications

You are asked to add a card and set up Apple Pay. Then you will be walked through setting up features such as Activity, SOS, & automatic watchOS updates. You can setup cellular on cellular models.

You will now be able to install applications that are supported by the Apple Watch, or you can choose to install them later.

Allow your devices to synchronize

Depending on the amount of information you have, the syncing may take a long time.

Ensure your devices are near each other till you hear a chime & feel a tap from your watch, then press the Digital Crown.

SETUP A FAMILY MEMBER'S WATCH

You can setup and manage a watch for someone that does not have an iPhone, such as your children or your parents. To do this, you have to be a guardian/parent or the family organizer in your Family Sharing group.

After setting up the person's watch you can use the Watch application & Screen Time on your Phone to manage the following:

- ❖ Communication limit
- ❖ Time away from the screen Schedule
- ❖ School time-a feature that helps to limit certain features of the Apple Watch during school hours
- ❖ Calendar & Mail settings for Gmail & iCloud accounts
- ❖ Restrictions on content, purchases, and privacy

You can also view Location, Health, & Activity information of the managed watch based on how you setup the watch.

- ❖ Tell the person to wear their watch
- ❖ Switch on the watch by long-pressing the side button till you see the Apple symbol.

❖ Ensure your Phone is close to the watch, wait for the pairing screen of your watch to show on your Phone, and click the Continue button.

Otherwise, enter the Watch application on your Phone, click on the **All Watches** button, and touch Pair New Watch.

❖ Click the **Setup for a Family Member** button, and click the Continue button on the next screen.

❖ When asked, place your Phone in a way that your watch appears in the view finder in the Watch application. It would pair the 2 devices.

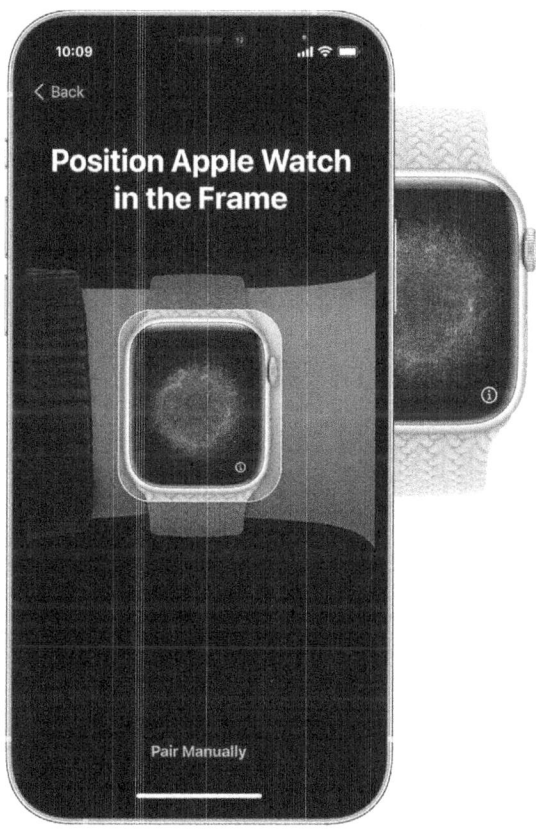

❖ Click the **Setup Apple Watch** button. Adhere to the directives on your Phone and watch to complete the setup.

Manage a family's members watch

❖ Enter the Watch application on the Phone you are using to manage the watch.
❖ Click on **All Watches**, click on a watch in the **Family Watches** section then touch Done.

BASICS

Apple Watch Series 7

The images below would help you get started with using the Apple Watch Series 7

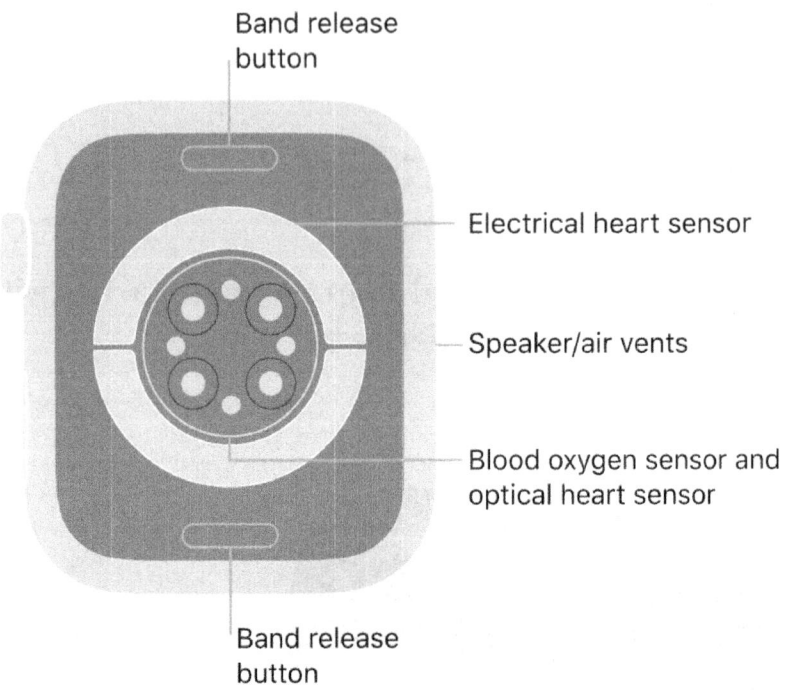

Apple Watch gestures

You use a few gestures to interact with your Apple Watch.

Tap: Use a finger to touch your screen gently.

Swipe: Move a finger across your display- left, down, up, or right.

Drag: Move a finger across your display without raising it.

Watch app

Use the Watch application on your iPhone to personalize watch faces, change settings & notifications, install applications, etc.

To open your Apple Watch application, simply adhere to the directives below:

- Touch the Watch application icon on your iPhone.

- Touch **My Watch** to see your watch's settings.

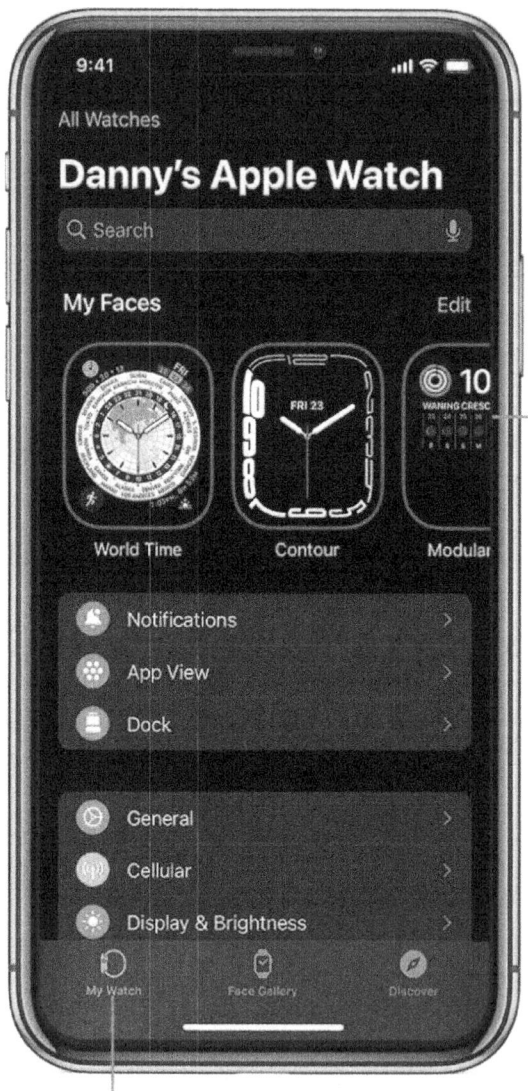

Swipe to see your watch face collection.

Settings for Apple Watch.

Charge your Apple Watch

Setup the charger

❖ Place the charger or charging cord on a flat surface in a well-ventilated area.

The Apple Watch Series 7 comes with an Apple Watch Magnetic Fast Charger to USB-C cable.

❖ Insert the charging cable into the power adapter.
❖ Connect the adapter to the power outlet.

Start charging your Watch

Put the Apple Watch Magnetic Charger on the back of the Apple Watch. The concave end of the charger would snap to the back of your watch and would align neatly.

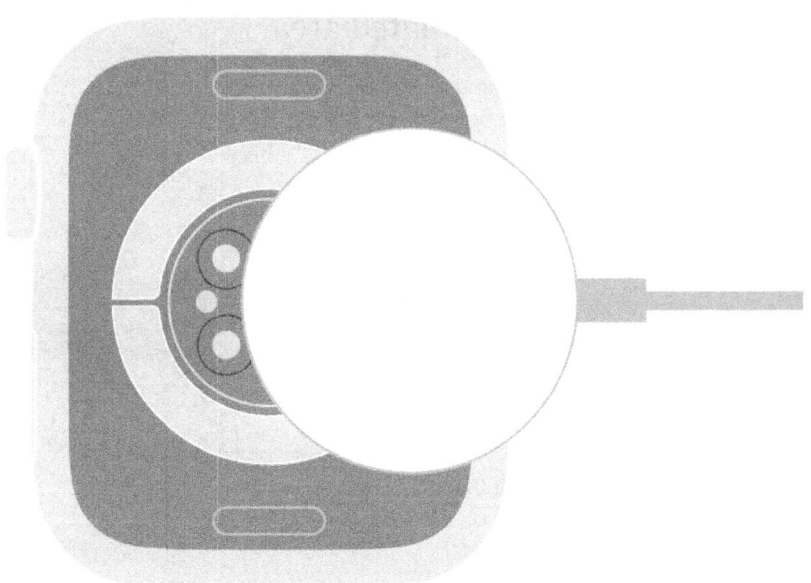

When charging your watch, you would hear a sound (unless your Watch is in silent mode) and see a charge icon⚡ on your watch's face. The Apple Watch turns red when power is needed, and the Apple Watch turns green when charged.

You can charge your watch in a flat position or on its side.

To see the remaining power, simply long-press the bottom of your watch display and swipe up to open the Controls Centre.

Save power when your watch battery is low

You can put your device in Power Reserve mode to extend battery life. The Apple Watch still shows time, but you cannot utilize applications.

❖ Long press the bottom of your display, then swipe up to open the Controls Centre.
❖ Touch the battery percentage, and slide the Power Reserve slide to the right.

To go back to Normal Power mode, simply restart your watch by long-pressing the Side button till you see the Apple symbol. You must have more than 10% charge for your device to restart

How to open applications on your watch

The Apple Watch comes with different applications that can help you monitor your health, exercise, etc. To launch applications, simply press the Digital Crown, then touch the application. Press the Digital Crown once more to go back to your Watch's Home Screen. You can download more applications from the Application Store on your Watch.

Always On feature

The Always-On feature allows your device to show the watch-face & time, even when you put your wrist down. When you raise your hand, your device would function fully.

- ❖ Enter the Setting application on your watch.
- ❖ Touch Display and Brightness, then click on Always on.
- ❖ Activate **Always On**, then click on the following options to configure them:
  - Display Complications Data: Select the Complications that display info when you put your wrist down.
  - Show Notification: Select notifications that appear when you put your wrist down.
  - Show Apps: Select applications that remain visible when you put your wrist down.

Wake your Watch display

As a rule, you can wake up the Apple Watch display in the following ways:

- Raise your hand. Your watch would sleep again when you put your wrist down.
- Tap your screen, or click the Digital Crown.

- Rotate the digital crown upwards.

If you don't want the Apple Watch to wake up when you lift your wrist or rotate the Digital Crown, simply enter the Settings application on your Watch, head over to **Display and Brightness**, then configure Wake on **Wrist Raise**.

Go back to the clock face

You can decide how long before your Watch goes back to the clock face from an open application.

- Enter the watch's Settings application.
- Head over to General, touch Return to Clock, then scroll down and select the time you want your watch to go back to the clock face.

You can also press the Digital Crown to go back to the clock face.

Wake up to your last activity

For some applications, you can configure the Apple Watch to take you back to where you were before the watch went to sleep. These applications include Workout, Mindfulness, Walkie-Talkie, Voice

Memos, Stopwatch, Play Now, Podcasts, Timers, Music, Maps, & Audiobooks.

- Enter the Settings application on your Watch.
- Head over to General, touch **Return to Clock**, scroll down, and touch an application, then activate **Return to Application**.

You can also open the Watch application on your iPhone, touch the **My Watch** button, and then head over to General> Return to Clock.

Keep the Apple Watch screen on longer

You can keep your Watch screen on longer when you touch to wake your watch.

- Launch the Settings application on your Watch.
- Touch **Display and Brightness**, touch **Wake Duration**, and touch **Wake for 70 seconds**.

Select a language or region

- Launch the Watch application on your Phone.
- Touch **My Watch**, head over to **General**, tap on **Language and Region**, touch the **Custom** button, and click on Watch Language.

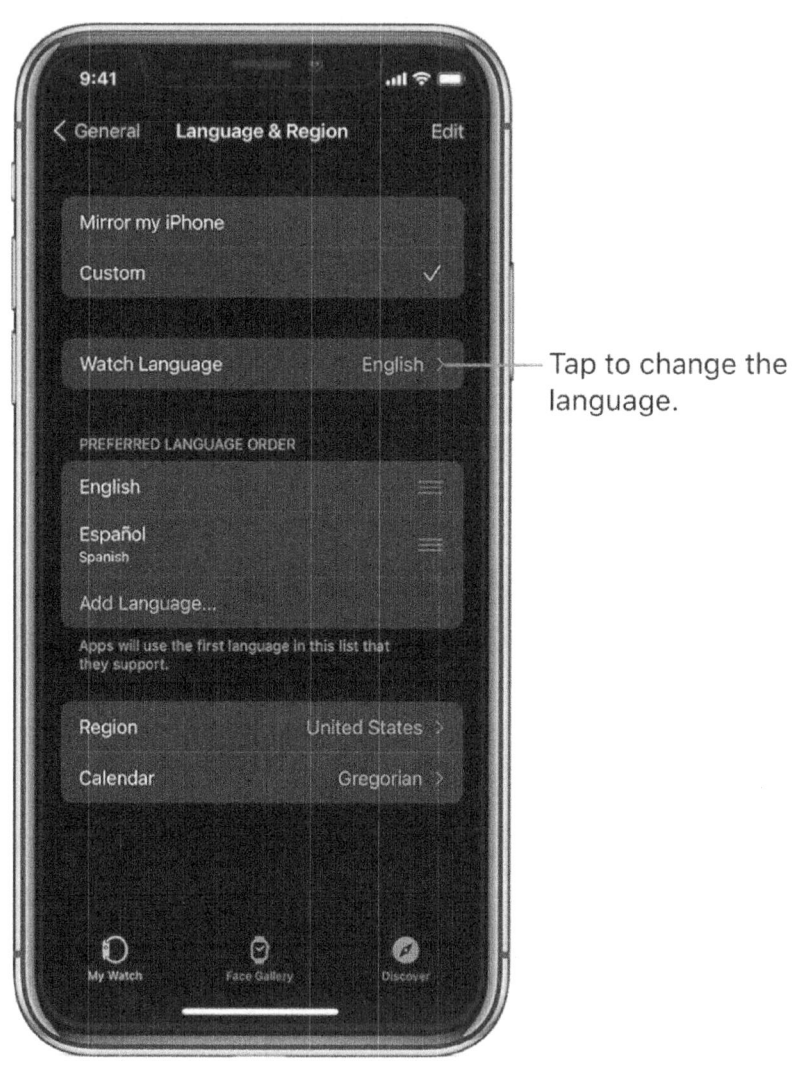

Tap to change the language.

Change Wrist or digital Crown orientation

If you want to transfer your Watch to your other hand or you prefer the Digital Crown on the other side, change your orientation settings so that raising your hand would wake your watch, and rotating the digital crown would move things in the direction you want.

❖ Launch the Settings application on your Watch.
❖ Head over to General, then touch Orientation.

You can as well launch the Watch application on your iPhone, touch My Watch, and head over to General> Watch Orientation.

Apple Watch control screen. You can customize your wrists and wristbands with Crown Digital.

Calculate a tip & split the check

- Enter the Calculator application on your watch.
- Enter the total amount of the bill & click on Tip.
- Rotate the digital crown to select a tip percentage.
- Touch People, rotate the Digital Crown to enter the number of individuals that are going to share the bill.
  You will see the tip, the total amount, and how much each individual owes.

Set a timer

The Timer application on your watch can help you to keep track of time.

❖ Launch the Timers application on your watch.
❖ Click the time limit to start the timer.
❖ Scroll down to select a custom or recent time.

When the timer expires, you can touch the Repeat button to start another timer of that duration.

While the timer is counting you can Pause it by tapping the Pause button, touching the Play button to continue counting, or touching the cancel button to end the session

Get directions on your watch

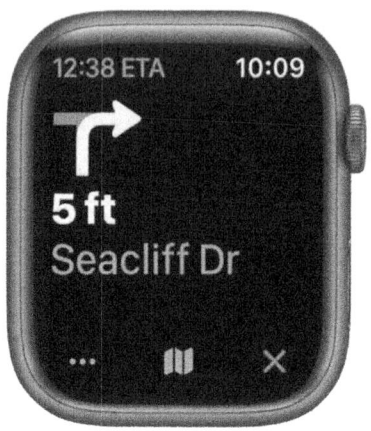

- Enter the Maps application on your watch.
- Rotate the Digital Crown to navigate to Recents, Guides, Favorites.
- Touch an entry to receive cycling, transit, walking, or driving, directions.
- Click on a mode to see the directions provided, then click on a route to start your journey and see an overview with turns, turn distances & street names.
Look in the upper left corner to see when you will arrive.

Adjust the text size

You can adjust the text size that appears in any area that is compatible with Dynamic View, such as the Setting application.

- Enter the Settings application on your watch.

- Head over to Display and Brightness> Text Size, then rotate the Digital Crown to change it.

Restart your watch

- Switch off your watch: Long-press your watch's side button till the sliders show up, then slide the Power Off slider to the right.
- Switch on your watch: Long-press the side button till the Apple symbol shows up.

Forces restart your watch

If you cannot switch off your watch or if the problem persists, you can force restart your watch. This should only be done if you cannot restart your watch.

To force restart your watch, press & hold the Digital Crown & the Side button simultaneously for a minimum of 10 seconds till the Apple symbol shows on your screen.

Erase your watch & settings

- ❖ Enter the Settings application on your watch.
- ❖ Head over to General> Reset, touch Erase All Content & Settings, and enter your code.
  If you own a watch with a cellular plan, you have two options - Delete All and Delete All and Keep Plan.

You can also launch the Watch application on your Phone, click on the My Watch button, head over to General> Reset, and click on Erase Apple Watch Setting & Contents.

If you cannot access the Setting application on your watch because you forgot the passcode of your watch, put your watch on its charger, and hold down the power button till Power Off is displayed on your screen. Long-press the Digital Crown, and touch the Reset button.

Backup your watch

Your watch is automatically backed up to the phone it's paired with and can be restored from a backup. When you back your Phone to iCloud or Mac or PC, the Apple Watch backup is added. If your backups are stored in iCloud, you won't be able to view their contents.

Update the software of your watch

You can update the Apple Watch software by checking for updates in the watch application on your phone.

- ❖ Launch the Watch application on your Phone
- ❖ Click on My Watch, head over to General> Software Updates, and if there is an update, click Download & Install.

CUSTOMIZE YOUR WATCH

Display your applications in a list or on a grid

The Home Screen can show application programs in a grid or list. To choose one, adhere to the guidelines below:

1. Long-press the Home Screen.

2. Select list or grid view.

You can also launch the Settings application on your Watch, touch App View, and touch Grid View.

Launch applications from the Home Screen

How you launch an application depends on the view you are making use of.

Grid view: Touch the application icon. If you are already looking at the Home Screen, you can rotate the Digital Crown to launch the application in the middle of your screen.

List view: Rotate the Digital Crown, and touch any application.

To go back to the Home screen from an application, press the Digital Crown, then press the Digital Crown once more to go to the watch face (or click on the clock icon ⌣ on the Home screen in grid format).

Double-click the Digital Crown to quickly open the last application you used while using another application or Watch Face.

Re-arrange your applications in grid format

1. Press your watch's Digital Crown to go to the Home screen.
   If the screen is in list format, long-press your Home screen, and then touch the Grid View button. Or, launch the Settings application on your Watch, touch App View, and touch Grid View.
2. Long-press an application icon, and then touch the Edit Apps button.
3. Move an application to another location by dragging it.
4. Click the digital crown when you are done.

Touch and hold an app, then drag to a new location.

Otherwise, launch the Apple Watch application on your iPhone, touch **My Watch**, click on **App View**, and touch the **Arrangement** button. Long-press an application icon, then move it to another location by dragging it.

Note: In list format, applications are always arranged alphabetically.

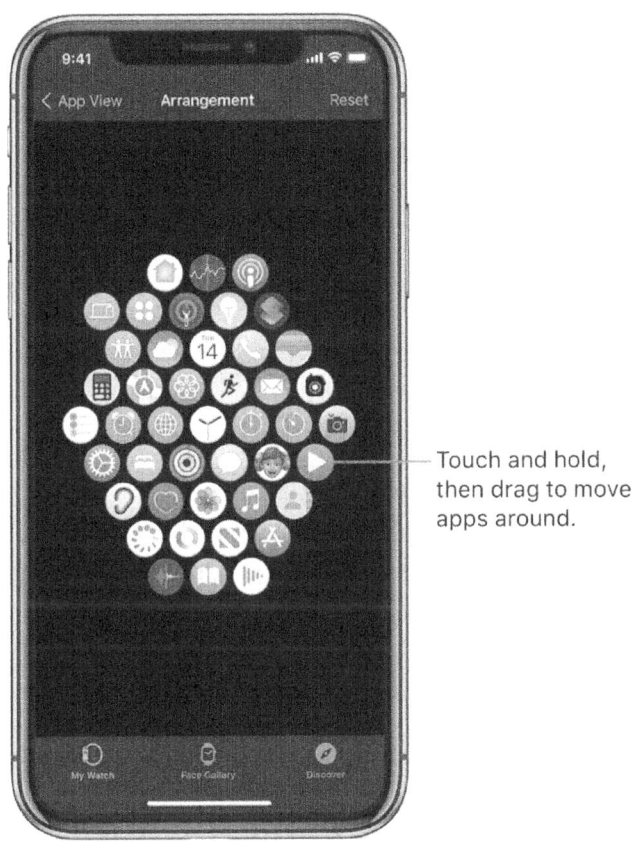

Touch and hold, then drag to move apps around.

Remove an application from your Watch

In Grid view, simply long-press the home screen, touch **Edit Apps**, and then click on the **X** to remove the application from your Watch. The application would stay on your paired Phone unless you erased it there as well.

In List format, you can just swipe the application to the left, then touch the Delete icon to remove the application from your watch.

Note: Not all applications can be removed from your watch.

Make changes to the application settings

- Launch the Watch application on your Phone.
- Click on **My Watch**, then scroll down to view the applications you have installed.
- Click on an application to change its layout.

See the storage space an application is using

You can learn how your watch storage space is being utilized.

- Head over to the Settings application on your watch.
- Head over to General, then click on storage.

You can also launch Apple Watch on your Phone, touch My Watch, and go to General> Storage.

Download an Application Store on your Watch

1. Open the App Store application ⊕ on your Watch.
2. Rotate the Digital Crown to view specific applications.
   Touch any category or touch **See All** below a collection to view more applications.
3. Touch **Get** if you want to get a free application. Click on the price to purchase an application.

If a Download icon ⬇ is displayed on the application instead of the price, it means that you have already bought the application and can download it again for free.

Click the Search field at the top of your watch display to find a specific application, then type or use dictation or Scribble to type the name of the application.

Install applications you already have on your iPhone

As a rule, the applications on your Phone that have watchOS applications available are automatically installed & would show on your watch Home Screen. Adhere to the directives below to learn how to choose to install specific applications:

1. Enter the Watch application on your Phone.
2. Touch **My Watch**, then touch General, and disable **Automatic App Install**.
3. Click on **My Watch**, then scroll to the Available Applications.
4. Touch the Install button next to the applications you plan on installing.

Tell time on your Watch

There are many ways to tell time with your Watch.

1. **Lift your hand:** The time would appear on your watch face.
2. **Hear the Time:** enter the Settings application on your Watch, touch the **Clock** button, and activate **Speak Time**. Hold 2 of your fingers on your watch face to hear the time.
   The Apple Watch can play chimes on the hour. In the Apple Watch Settings application, click the **Clock** button and activate **Chimes**. Touch **Sounds** to pick Birds or Bells.
3. **Feel the time:** To feel the time tapped out on your hand when your watch is in silent mode, launch the Apple Watch **Settings** application, touch the **Clock** button, click on **Taptic Time**, activate **Taptic Time**, and select an option.
   Note: If Taptic Time is deactivated, your Watch might speak the time. To use Taptic Time, first enter the Settings application, touch Clock, and activate **Control with Silent mode** in Speak Time segment.
   Utilize Siri: lift your hand and say, "What time is it?"

Open or close the Control Center

The Controls Centre is an easy way to view your battery percentage, mute your smartwatch, pick a

Focus, turn your Watch into a flash light, put your Smartwatch in Airplane mode, etc.

1. Open the Control Centre: simply swipe up from your watch face. From another screen, long-press the bottom of your display, and drag it up.
Note: You cannot open the Controls Centre on the Apple Watch Home screen. Instead, click the Digital Crown to launch an application or go to the watch face, then open the Controls Centre.
2. Close the Controls Centre: Swipe down from the top of your display, or click the Digital Crown.

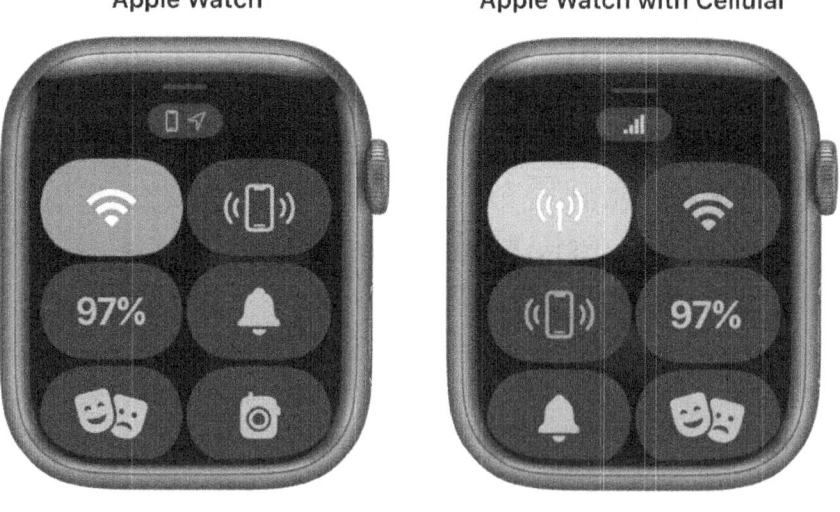

Touch and hold the bottom, then swipe up to open Control Center.

Change the Control Centre arrangement

You can rearrange the Controls Centre buttons by adhering to the guidelines below:

1. Open the Control Center, scroll to the end of the Controls Centre, then click on the Edit button.
2. Drag any button to another location.
3. Touch Done when you are through.

Remove things from the control centre

You can remove things from the Control Centre by adhering to the directives below:

1. Open the Control Center, scroll to the end of the Controls Centre, then click on the Edit button.
2. Touch the Remove icon in the corner of the item you plan to erase.
3. Touch the Done button when you are done.

To bring back a removed button, open the Controls Centre, touch the Edit button, and click on the Add button close to the button you want to return. Touch Done when you are through.

Theater mode

The Theater mode stops the display of your Watch from turning on when you lift your hand. It also activates Silent mode & makes disables your Walkie-Talkie status, but you still get instant notifications.

Open the Control Centre, touch the Theater Mode button, and then click Theater mode.

Turn theater mode on or off.

When theater mode is active, you will see a theater mode indicator at the top of your display.

Find your iPhone

The Apple Watch can help you look for your Phone if it's close.

Open the Controls Centre, and press the Ping iPhone button .

Your Phone would make a sound that allows you to look for it.

Tip: In the dark? Long-Press the Ping Phone button and your Phone would flash as well.

Adjust the brightness & text on your Watch

On the Apple Watch, open the Settings application and touch the **Display and Brightness** button to change the below:

❖ Brightness: Touch the Brightness controls to change the brightness or touch the slider, then rotate the Digital Crown.
❖ Size of text: Click on **Text Size**, then touch the letters or rotate the Digital Crown.
❖ Bold text: activate Bold Text.

You can also make these changes on your Phone. Launch the Watch application on your Phone, touch **My Watch**, touch the **Display and Brightness** button, and then change the text & brightness.

Adjust your watch volume

- Enter the Settings application on your Watch.
- Touch the **Sounds and Haptic** button.
- Touch the volume controls below Alert Volume, or touch the slider, then rotate the Digital Crown to adjust the volume.

Alternatively, open the **Watch application** on your Phone, touch the **Sounds and Haptic** button, and slide the Alert Volume slider.

You can also lower the volume of the headphones connected to your Watch. In the settings application, touch **Sound and Haptic**> Headphone Safety, and activate Reduce Loud Sound.

Adjust the haptic strength of your Watch

You can adjust the intensity of the haptics or the wrist taps you watch utilizes for alerts & notifications.

❖ Enter the Settings application on your Watch.
❖ Touch **Sounds and Haptic**, and activate Haptic Alerts.
❖ Select Prominent or Default.

Alternatively, launch the Watch application on your Phone, touch **My Watch**, touch the **Sounds and Haptic** button, and select Prominent or Default.

Activate or Deactivate Digital Crown haptics

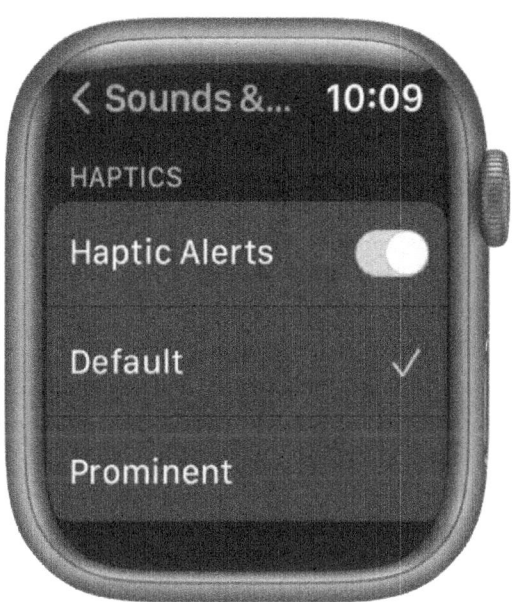

On your Apple Watch Series 7, you feel clicks when you rotate the Digital Crown to scroll. To activate or deactivate this haptics, adhere to the guidelines below:

❖ Enter the Settings application on your Watch.
❖ Touch **Sound and Haptic**, then activate or deactivate Crown Haptic.

Alternatively, launch the Watch application on your Phone, touch **My Watch**, touch **Sounds and Haptic**, and activate Crown Haptics.

Reply to a message when it arrives

1. If you feel or hear an alert, lift your hands to check it out.
2. Rotate the Digital Crown to navigate to the bottom of the message, and touch a button there. You can also touch the application icon in the notification to open the corresponding app.
3. Swipe down to clear a message. Otherwise, go to the end of the message, and then touch the Dismiss button.

Manage your Apple ID settings with your Watch

You can view and edit Apple ID-related information on WatchOS 8. Add & edit your profile, make changes to your login code, add a secure phone number, etc.

- ❖ Head over to the Settings application on your Watch.
- ❖ Touch [your user name].
- ❖ Touch Name, Phone Number, E-mail, Subscription or Password & Security, and change whatever you want

Create an emergency Medical ID

A Medical ID provides info that may be important in an emergency, such as your medical condition & allergies. You Watch can provide this info, so that it is available for the individual attending to you in an emergency.

- ❖ Open the health application on your Phone.
- ❖ Touch your Profile picture at the upper right part of your display, and touch the Medical ID button.
- ❖ Touch the Get Started button, and enter your info.

View your medical profile on your Watch

- ❖ Press your Watch side button till the sliders appear
- ❖ Move the Medical ID slider to the right by sliding it.

If you can't find your Medical ID when you long-press the Side button, launch the **Watch** application on your Phone, click **My Watch**, click on the **Health** button, click on **Medical ID**, click **Edit**, then activate **Show When Locked**. To hide your medical information when the Apple Watch is locked, deactivate Show when locked.

Connect your Watch to Wi-Fi

By connecting your Watch to WiFi, you can continue to utilize many of your watch's features, even if you don't have an iPhone with you.

❖ Open the Control Centre.

❖ Long-press the WiFi button and then touch the name of the available WiFi network.
The Wi-Fi system compatible with your Watch is 802.11b / g / n 2.4GHz.

❖ If a password is needed to connect to the network, do any of the below:
  ➢ Use the QWERTY keyboard on the Apple Watch to enter the password.

  ➢ Click the password button , then select a password from the list.

➢ Utilize your finger to scribble the login code characters on your screen. Use the Digital Crown to select small & capital letters.
➢ Use the keyboard on your Phone to insert the login code.
❖ Click Join.

Connect your Watch to headphones or Bluetooth speakers

Play songs from your watch on Bluetooth speakers or headphones.

Tip: If you have AirPods that you have setup with your iPhone, just click play.

Adhere to the directives that came with your speaker or headset to place them in discovery mode. When the Bluetooth device is ready, follow the directives below:

❖ Open your watch's Settings application and touch Bluetooth.
❖ Touch the device when it shows up.

You can also touch the AirPlay button on the play screen in Podcasts, Now Playing, Music, &

Audiobooks applications to enter the Bluetooth setting.

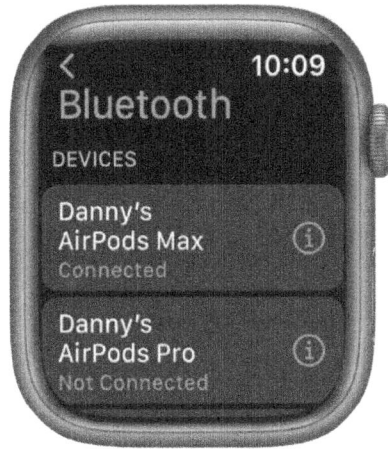 

Monitor the volume of your headphone

❖ Open the Control Centre.
❖ Touch the **Edit** button and touch the Add button beside the headset button to add it.
❖ When you listen to headphones that are connected to your Watch, open the Controls Centre and touch the headset sound button .
A meter indicates the current volume of your headphone.

Handoff Tasks from your watch

The Hand-off feature allows you to move from one device to another without forgetting what you are doing. For instance, you can start replying to an email in the Mail application on your Watch, and finish answering the e-mail on your iPhone. The Handoff feature is only available in Apple watch you setup for yourself, but not the one you setup for a family member. Adhere to the directives below to utilize Handoff.

❖ Open your iPhone.

❖ On a Face ID iPhone, swipe up from the bottom edge & stop to display the Application Switcher. (On iPhones with a Home button, double-click the Home button to display the Application Switch.)

❖ Touch the button that shows at the end of the screen to open the same thing on your iPhone.

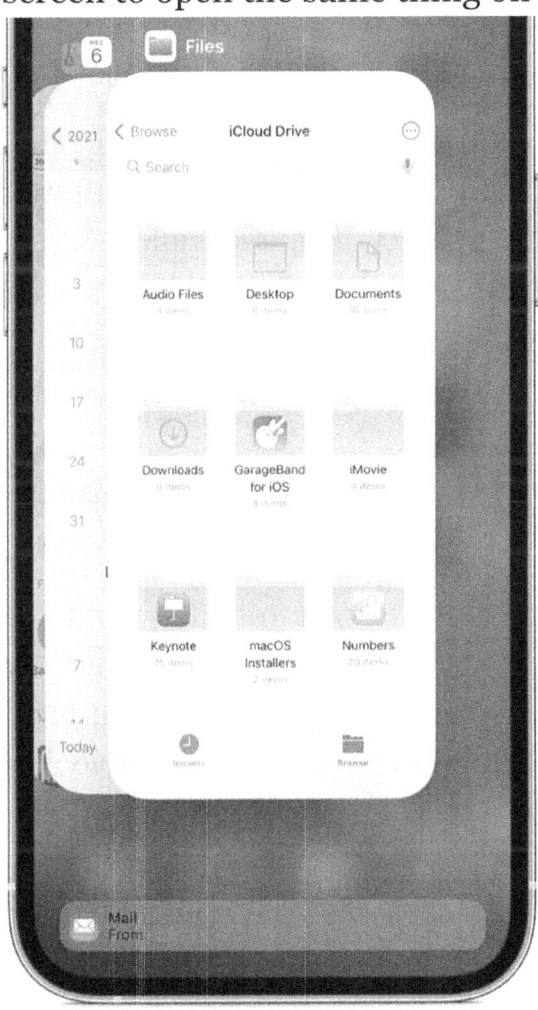

Tip: If you don't see a button on the Application switcher, ensure Handoff is activated on your iPhone in Settings> General> AirPlay and Handoff.

The Handoff feature is enabled by default. To deactivate it, launch the Watch application on your iPhone, touch My Watch, touch General, and deactivate **Enable Handoff**.

The Handoff feature works with Siri, alarm, settings, calendar, messages, mail, weather, Home, podcasts, Maps, Stocks, News, music, stopwatch, phone, reminders, activity, timers, wallet, & global clock. In order for Handoff to work, the Apple Watch must be connected to a paired iPhone.

Use your Apple Watch to unlock your Mac

If you own a MacOS 10.13 or later Mac (mid -2013 or after), your Watch can unlock your Mac immediately when it wakes from sleep. You have to be logged in to iCloud with the same Apple ID on your Apple Watch & Mac.

Activate Auto-Unlock

1. Adhere to the guidelines below to setup your device:

- ➢ The WiFi & Bluetooth of your Mac is activated.
- ➢ Your Apple Watch & Mac are logged in to iCloud with the one Apple ID, and your Apple ID is making use of 2-factor authentication.
- ➢ Your Watch is making use of a pass-code.

2. On your MacBook or iMac, select the **Apple menu**, and then click **System Preference**.
3. Click on the **Security and Privacy** button, and click on **General**.

4. Choose **Use the Apple Watch to open applications and your Mac**, or **Allow your Watch open your Mac**."

If you own more than one Apple Watch, choose the watch you want to utilize to open your applications & Mac.

If your Apple ID does not have two-factor authentication, adhere to the directives on your display, and select the check box once more.

Open your Mac

While putting on your watch, simply wake up your Mac - you don't have to enter your login code.

Tip: Ensure your Watch is on your wrist & open and you are close to your Mac.

Unlock your iPhone with your Watch

While putting on your Watch, you can utilize it to safely open your Phone (Face ID models) when putting on a Face mask.

To unlock your Phone with your Watch, adhere to the directives below:

1. On your iPhone, enter the **Settings** application, touch **Face ID and Passcode,** and type your login code.
2. Scroll down and activate **Apple Watch** (in the **Unlock with Apple Watch** segment).
If you own many watches, activate the setting for each one.
3. To open your Phone while putting on a Face mask, just ensure you are putting on your Apple Watch, wake your iPhone, and then look at the screen.
Your watch would tap your hand to let you know that your Phone has been opened.

Note: If you want to unlock your iPhone, you must have a passcode on your Watch, your watch also has to be unlocked on your wrist, and it must be near your Phone.

Turn cellular on or off

The Apple Watch makes use of the best available network connection. You can enable or disable cellular - to save battery power, for example. Simply adhere to the directives below:

- Open the Controls Centre.
- Touch the cell button ((•)), then enable or disable Cellular.

If the Apple Watch has a cell connection and your iPhone is not close, the cell button will turn green.

Set an alarm on your watch

Utilize the Alarm application to vibrate or play a sound on your watch at a specific time.

- Open the Alarm application ⏻ on your watch.
- Touch the **Add Alarm** button.
- Press AM or PM, then click the minutes or hours. This procedure is not necessary when making use of 24-hour time.
- Rotate the digital crown to adjust, then click the Check button ✓.
- Click its switch to turn the alarm off or on. Or, touch the alarm time to set snooze, label, & repeat options.

To delete an alarm, simply enter the Alarm application ⊙, click on the Alarm in the list, scroll down and touch the **Delete** button

HOW TO CHANGE THE APPLE WATCH BAND

First thing is to ensure that you are using the band size that matches the case of your Apple Watch.

1. Put the face of your watch down in a clean place, such as a micro-fiber cloth or a soft padded mat.
2. If you own a Link Bracelet, press the Release button on a link to separate the band.
3. Long-Press the release button of the band, then slide the band to remove it from your watch.

4. If the band does not slide-out, press the release button once more and ensure you hold down the button while removing the band.

5. Ensure the band text is facing you, and slide the new band till you hear & feel a click.

Solo Loop

If you own a Braided Solo Loop or Solo Loop, just drag from the band's bottom to extend the band over your wrist when putting it on and taking it off.

Milanese Loop

You can fully open the Milanese Loop band by sliding the magnetic block through the lug or band connector.

Remove the Link Bracelet

Before you remove the band from your Watch, you need to separate the Link Bracelet into 2 parts. When removing the band, do not twist or force the band. Adhere to the directives below to avoid damaging the clasp or band.

Close the closure of the butterfly

If it is open, fold in the closure 1 side at a time till you hear a click.

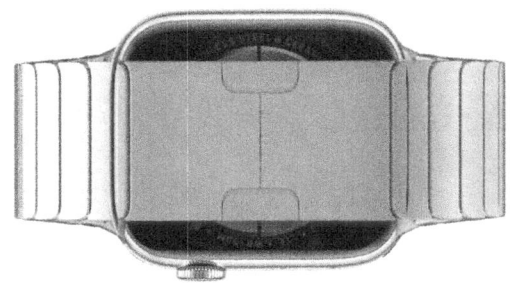

Long-Press the quick release key

The release keys are inside the bracelet. You just have to long-press one of the buttons.

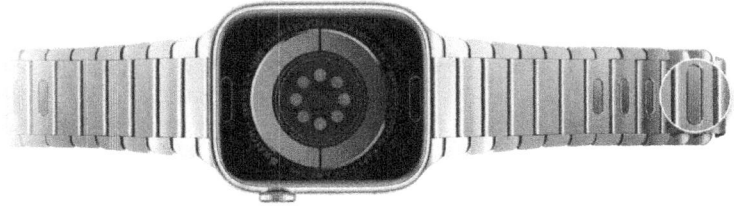

Remove the links gently

Long-press the release key while pulling. Separate the band into 2 pieces before you remove the band from your watch.

Remove the band

Long press the release button of your band and slide your watch band to remove it.

APPLE WATCH FACES

Customize your watch face from your iPhone

The Watch app's Face Gallery is the easiest way to view all the watch faces available. After finding a watch face that you like you can personalize it, select complications, and add the face to your collection.

Enter the Face Gallery

Enter the Watch application on your Phone, and click on Face Gallery.

Choose features for a watch face

Click on a face in your Face Gallery, then click on a feature like a style or colour.

When you play with different options, the top face changes to make sure the design is what you want.

Add complications in the Face Gallery

❖ Click on a face in the Face Gallery, and then touch a complication position, like Bottom, Top Right or Left.

- Swipe to view the available complications for the position you selected, and touch the one you like.
- If you don't want any complication to be in that position, scroll up and touch Off.

Add a face

- When you are done customizing a watch face in the Face Gallery, click the Add button.
- To go to the new watch face on your watch, simply swipe left across the watch face till you find it.

Customize the watch face from your Watch

The Watch application's Face Gallery is the simplest way to check out existing watch faces, edit one and add it to your collection. However, if your iPhone is not close to you, you can personalize the face on your watch.

Select a different watch face

- Swipe across the watch-face to view more faces in your collection.

❖ To view all watch-faces available, long-press the watch face, swipe to the face you like, and touch it.

Swipe left or right to see other watch faces.

Add features to your watch face.

Adding complications to a watch face

You can add features -known as complications- to some watch faces so that you can quickly see things like the weather reports, stock prices, or other info from other installed applications.

❖ With your watch face showing, long-press your screen, touch the Edit button.
❖ Swipe to the left till you get to the end.
If a watch face has complications, you can find them on the last screen.
❖ Click on a complication to select it, then rotate your watch's Digital Crown to pick a new one - For example Heart Rate or Activity.
❖ When you're done, press the Digital Crown to save the changes you have made, and touch the face to move to it.

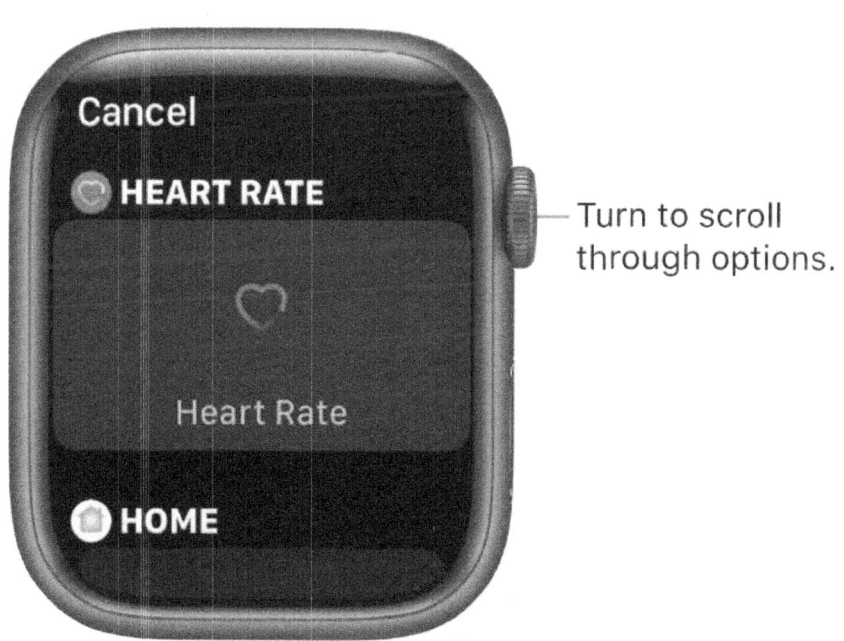

Turn to scroll through options.

Adding a watch face to your collection

Create a collection of unique faces, even variations of one design.

- ❖ With the watch face showing, long-press your screen.
- ❖ Swipe to the left till you get to the end, then touch the New (+) button.
- ❖ Rotate the Digital Crown to view watch faces, and click the Add button.
  Tip: Touch a collection like New in watchOS to view specific categories of watch faces.

After adding it, you can personalize the watch face.

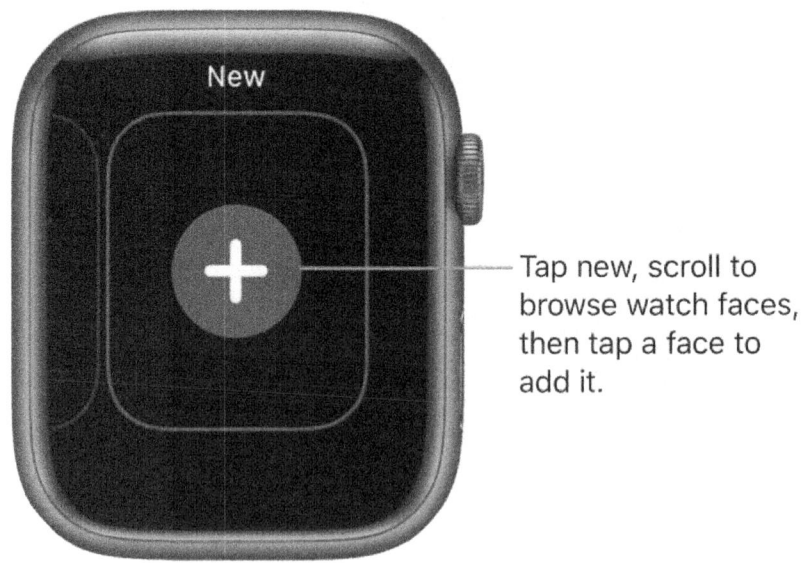

Tap new, scroll to browse watch faces, then tap a face to add it.

Check out your collection

❖ Enter the Watch application on your iPhone.
❖ Touch My Watch, and swipe through the collection in the **My Faces** segment.

You can rearrange your collection's order by tapping the Edit button and dragging ═ beside a watch face down or up.

Deleting a face from your collection

❖ With the watch face showing, long-press your screen.
❖ Swipe to the shape you don't like, then delete it by swiping it up.

Swipe up to delete a watch face, then tap Remove.

Otherwise, launch the Apple Watch application on your Phone, touch **My Watch**, and click the Edit button in the My Faces segment. Click the remove button ➖ beside the watch faces you plan on removing, then touch the Remove button.

Set your watch ahead

❖ Enter the Settings application on your Watch.
❖ Touch the Clock button.
❖ Tap +0 min, then rotate the Digital Crown to move the clock up to fifty-nine minutes ahead.

This setting only changes the time displayed on your watch face, it does not affect alarms, notification times, or other times like the World Clock.

Share and receive a Watch face

Your watch faces can be shared with friends. Shared faces may include complications that were added in watchOS and also the ones you created by third parties.

Note: The watch face receiver must have a watchOS 7 or after Apple Watch.

❖ Specify the watch face you want to share on the Apple Watch.
❖ Long press your screen and then click the Share button ⬆.
❖ Touch the name of the watch face, and touch the **"Don't Add"** button for the complications you do not want to share.
❖ Touch a Recipient, or click Mail or Messages.
If you click Messages or Mail, add contacts, subject (Mail), & messages.
❖ Click Send.

You can also launch the Watch application on your phone, click on a watch face from your Face Gallery or collection and touch the Share button ⬆️, then select a way to share it.

Receive a watch face

You can get the watch faces that were sent to you in Mail, Messages, or by tapping on a link online.

- ❖ Open the e-mail, text, email, or link that has the shared watch face.
- ❖ Touch the watch face, and click on the Add button.

FOCUS

The Focus mode is designed to help you stay focused when you want to concentrate on a task. The Focus mode can help in reducing distractions – letting only notifications you want to come through- and allow other individuals & applications to know that you are busy.

You can pick the provided Focus modes – which includes, work, sleep, personal, & driving. You can also create your own Focus on your Phone and choose who can contact you, which applications can send messages to you, and if you can receive time-sensitive notifications when the Focus mode is activated.

Note: If you want to share your focus options on all of your devices that you sign in with the same Apple ID, enter the Settings application> Focus, go to the bottom of your display, and activate **Share Across Devices**.

Activate or deactivate a Focus

❖ Open the Controls Centre.

❖ Long-press the Focus button and then touch a Focus.

If there is no active Focus, the Control Centre would show the DND icon ☾.

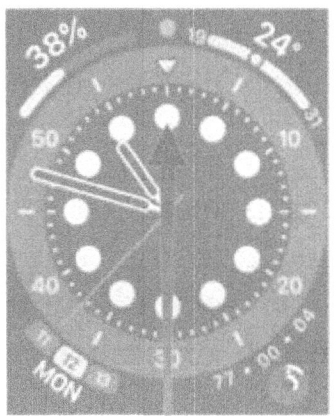 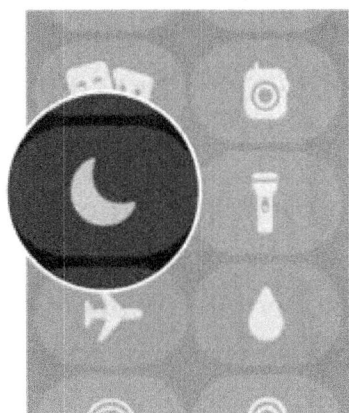

❖ Select an option for the Focus - On, On for an hour, On till tomorrow morning, or On till I leave.

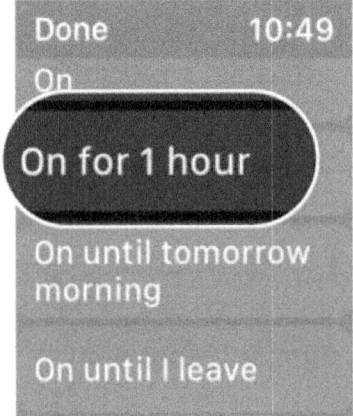

Press the Focus button in the Controls Centre to disable a Focus mode.

If a Focus is active, the icon of the Focus shows at the upper part of your watch face.

Create your Focus

❖ On your Phone, enter the Settings application, touch **Focus**.

❖ Touch the Add button ＋, select a Focus, and adhere to the directives on your screen.

Create a Focus schedule

You can set a Focus mode to activate at different times of the day. For instance, you can set the Work Focus mode to automatically activate at 9a.m. & end at 5PM, Monday through Friday.

❖ Enter your Watch's setting application.
❖ Touch **Focus**, touch the Focus you want to set a schedule for.

- ❖ Click the **Add New** button

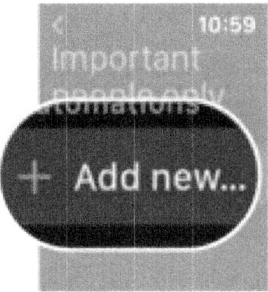

- ❖ Touch the **From** & **To** fields to set the start and end times.

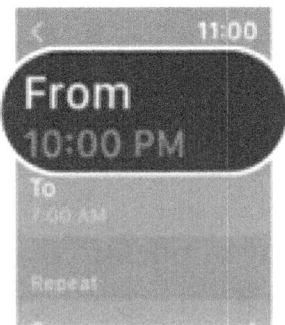 

- ❖ Scroll up and select the days you want the Focus mode to be active.

❖ In the upper left corner of your screen, touch <to save the Focus.
❖ Repeat this step to add more activity to the Focus.

Deactivate or delete a Focus schedule

To delete or deactivate a Focus schedule, do any of the below:

❖ **Deactivate a Focus schedule:** enter the Settings application on your Watch, touch Focus, and then touch a Focus. Touch a Schedule, scroll, and deactivate **Enabled**.

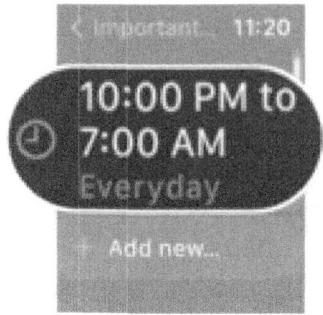 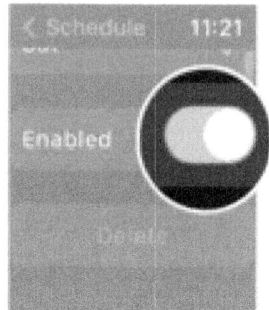

Activate **Enabled** when you want to turn on the schedule again.

❖ Delete a Focus Schedule: Enter the Watch's Settings application, click **Focus**, and then click on a Focus. Click a **Schedule**, scroll, and click the Delete button.

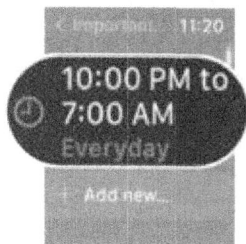 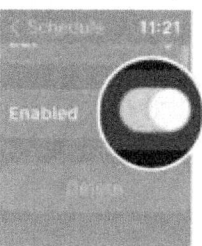 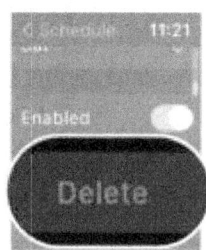

WORKOUT APP

The Workout application on your Watch provides tools to help you manage your individual workout sessions. You can set goals, such as calories, distance, or time, and your watch keeps track of your progress and sums up your results. You can also setup an exercise that includes a number of activities like running, swimming, and cycling. You can also make use of the Fitness application on your Phone to review your full workout history.

Start a workout

- Launch the Workout application on your Watch.
- Rotate your watch's Digital Crown to go to the workout you want.
  Touch the **Add Workout** button at the lower part of your display for sessions like surfing or kickboxing.
- Click the More button ••• to set a goal.

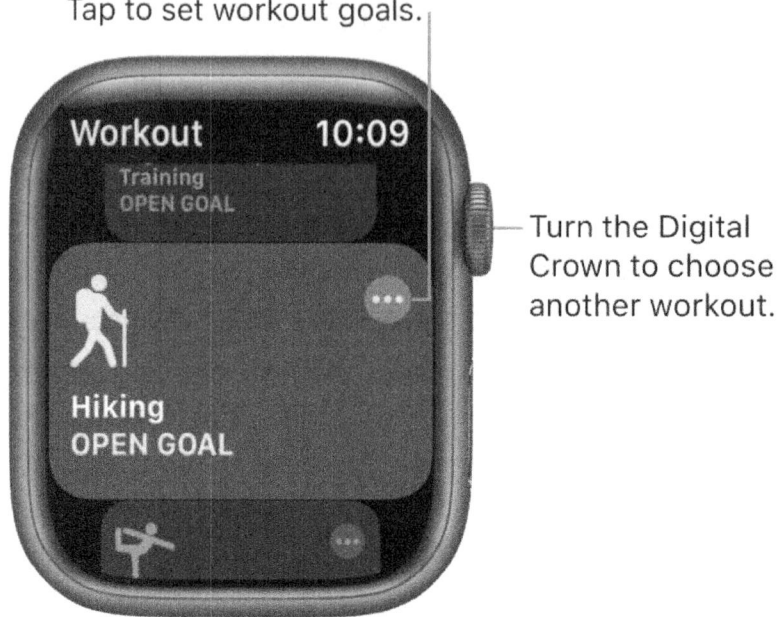

- ❖ Pick a distance, time, calorie, or open goal (which means that you didn't set a specific goal, but you still want your Watch to control your activity).
- ❖ Rotate the Digital Crown or touch + / - to set.
- ❖ When you are ready to go, click the Start button.

When you use the application and select an exercise, the sequence of exercises indicates your choice.

Tip: To start a workout without a goal, just click on the type of workout you want- a walk, stair stepper, or run.

Create a target speed for outdoor run exercises

Choose a target speed for an outdoor run, and the Apple Watch taps your wrist if you are running more than or behind the pace you chose after 1 mile.

❖ Launch the Workout application on your Watch.
❖ Rotate the Digital Crown to go to Outdoor Run, and touch the More button •••
❖ Touch Set alert, then touch the **OK** button.
❖ Set a time limit for running a mile - for example, 9 minutes - and press the Done button.

- Select Average or Rolling, and touch <.
  Average is your normal pace for all the miles you have run. Rolling is the speed of one mile taken at that time.

Your watch would remember the target you set across workouts. To change it, select Outdoor Run, click the More button ●●●, and then click on the current speed to change it.

Combine many activities in a single exercise

- Launch the Workout application on your Watch.
- Start your first workout, for example, outdoors run.
- When you are ready to begin another activity swipe right, touch the Add button ╂, and select an exercise.
- Once you are done with your workout session, swipe to the right and touch the End button.
- Rotate the Digital Crown to go through the summary of the results.
- Scroll down and touch the Done button to save the exercises.

Finish, pause, or lock your workout

- Swipe to the right, and touch the End icon ⊗ to end the workout.
- Swipe to the right, and touch the Pause icon ⏸ to pause the exercise. Or, press the Side button & the Digital Crown simultaneously. Press both buttons again to continue.
- You can lock the display to avoid accidental taps, simply swipe to the right, and touch the Lock button 💧. To unlock your display, simply rotate the Digital Crown.

Monitor your progress

Lift your wrist so that you can see how you are doing while working out. Then rotate your Digital Crown to show the metric that you want to see.

While running or walking, your Watch would tap you every kilometer or mile and it would show updates on the screen. If you are cycling, your watch would tap you every 5 kilometers or miles instead.

Edit the metrics for each exercise

- ❖ Launch Watch application on your Phone.
- ❖ Touch the **My Watch** tab, then touch Workout> Workout View.
- ❖ Click on **Multiple** or **Single** Metric.
  - ➢ If you select **Multiple Metrics**, you can select about 5 metrics per exercise. Click on a workout, and click on the Edit button. Delete or Add metrics, or long-press the Change Order icon to change the order.
  - ➢ If you select **Single Metric**, you can rotate the Digital Crown to go through all the metrics while working out.

Get reminders to start working out

When your watch notices that you are working out, it would tap your wrist & ask. Click on an option in the alert to record a workout, change the type of workout, mute the notification for that day, or turn off the notification.

The duration of your watch to record the exercise will vary depending on the type of exercise.

To activate or deactivate this feature, enter the Settings application on your Watch, touch **Workout**, and head over to Start Workout Reminder.

Get reminders to finish your workout

If your Watch notices that you are done working out, it would tap your wrist and ask. To pause or end the exercise, click the notification or dismiss the notification & continue working out.

To activate or deactivate this feature, launch the Settings application on your Watch, touch Workout, and head over to End Workout Reminder.

Activate DND

You can activate the Workout Do Not Disturb feature to automatically mute alerts & calls on your Watch when you start working out.

❖ Enter the Settings application on your Watch.
❖ Touch Do Not Disturb.
❖ Touch Workout Do Not Disturb.

When you are done working out, your watch will receive calls & alerts.

Save power while working

You can always use the Power Saver mode to turn off the heart rate sensor, Always On display & mobile data on your watch, to keep your battery life on runs & walks. The Apple Watch still counts active calories, distance, speed, and time spent.

To activate or deactivate Power Saver mode, adhere to the directives below:

❖ Launch the Watch application on your Phone.
❖ Touch the My Watch tab, and click on Workout.
❖ Activate or deactivate the power-saving mode.

Use gym equipment with your Watch

Your watch can synchronize & pair with compatible cardio equipment, like indoor bikes, ellipticals, treadmills, etc. which will give you more precise information about your workouts.

- Make sure the equipment is compatible – you will see "**Connect to Apple Watch**" on the equipment.
- Ensure your watch can detect the gym equipment – launch the Settings application on your Watch, click on Workout, and activate **Detect Gym Equipment**.
- Put your watch near the gym equipment's contactless reader, with the screen facing the reader.

  The soft tap & sound confirm that the Apple Watch is connected.

If the Detect Gym is turned off in Apple Watch settings, launch the Workout application, keep the Apple Watch close to the gym equipment, with the screen facing the reader.

To get started, click the Start button on the gym equipment. Click Stop on the equipment to end the exercise.

After completing your workout, the information from the gym equipment would appear in the workout summary in the Activity application on your Apple Watch and the Fitness application on your iPhone.

Start a swimming workout

- Enter the Workout application on your Watch.
- Choose Pool swim or Open water swim.

Press the Digital Crown & side button simultaneously to pause or resume your swim.

When you begin a swim workout, your Watch would automatically lock the screen with Water Lock to prevent accidental taps. When you are out of the water for a break or after you finish your workout, rotate the Digital Crown to open the screen and extract any water from the speaker. You hear a sound and you can feel the water on your waist.

To manually clear water when you are done swimming, just open the Controls centre, and touch the Water Lock button , then rotate the Digital Crown to open the screen and clean the water from the speakers.

Update your weight & height

- Launch the watch application on your phone.

- Click on **My Watch**, click Health> Health Detail, and touch the Edit button.
- Touch Weight or Height, then adjust.

The Watch makes use of the info you provide about your height, age, weight, sex, & disability to calculate the number of calories you burn, the distance you travel, and other information. The more you run with the Workout application, the more Apple Watch will learn about your fitness level and more accurately measure the calories you burn during aerobic activity.

The iPhone's GPS allows your Watch to achieve longer distance accuracy. For instance, if you carry your Phone when making use of the Workout application on a run, your watch would use the GPS of your phone to measure your stride. Then, if you do not carry your Phone or in places where GPS is not available, the Apple Watch would use the info stored to measure distance.

Apple Watch can use built-in GPS to track your movements.

Change the measurement units

If you like kilojoules to calories or meters to yards, you can change the measurement unit used in the workout application.

- Enter the Settings application on your Watch.
- Touch Workout, scroll down and click **Unit of Measure**.

Automatically pause running and cycling workout

- Enter the Settings application on your Watch.
- Click Workout and activate **Auto Pause**.

The Apple Watch would automatically pause and resume running and cycling exercises when you are crossing the street or drinking water.

FALL DETECTION

If your Apple Watch detects a hard fall while you are putting it on, it would tap your wrist, sound an alarm, and show a notification. You can either call emergency services or dismiss the alert by touching **I'm OK**, touching Close in the top left part, or clicking on the Digital Crown.

If your Watch senses that you are moving, it would wait for you to respond to the warning and would not automatically call emergency services. If your watch notices that you have not moved for about a minute, it will automatically call.

At the end of the call, your Apple watch would send a message to your emergency contacts with your location allowing them to know that a hard fall has been detected by your watch and that it has dialed emergency services. Your Apple watch would get your emergency contacts from your Medical ID.

Some regions & countries have many emergency service numbers. For these countries, the Apple Watch will call the number associated with ambulance services.

How to call

To call an emergency service, slide the Emergency SOS slider on the alert by sliding it.

How to end a call

After calling the emergency department, you can end the call when you are done or when you no longer need emergency help:

❖ Press the end key 🔴.

❖ On the End Call screen, touch Yes.

What happens if the Apple Watch detects that you are not moving

When the Apple Watch notices that you did not move for a minute, it starts counting for 30 seconds, tap you on your wrist & sound an alert. The alert would get louder so that you and others can hear the sound. If you do not want to call the emergency department, touch Cancel. Once the 30-seconds countdown is complete, the Apple Watch would automatically contact emergency service.

When the call connects, Apple Watch would play an emergency message to the emergency services informing them that it has detected a serious fall and then shares your location as longitude & latitude coordinates. If you have previously activated the **Share During Emergency Call** setting in your Medical ID, your Medical ID would be automatically shared with the emergency department. When the message is played for the first time, the sound is at full volume, but the sound is reduced so that you or someone close to you can talk to the emergency service personnel. The message would continue to play till you touch **Stop Recorded Message** or the end of the call.

Wrist Detection has to be activated for your watch to automatically call emergency services, to do this simply enter your watch's **settings** application, touch **Passcode**, and ensure that **Wrist Detection** is enabled.

When are falls recorded

Falls are recorded in the Health application automatically. If you want to check your fall history, enter the Health application on your phone, touch the Health Data tab, and click on Results.

Activate or deactivate fall detection

- Enter the Watch application on your phone and touch the **My Watch** tab.
- Touch **Emergency SOS**.
- Activate or deactivate Fall detection. After enabling fall detection, you can choose Always on or Only when working out.

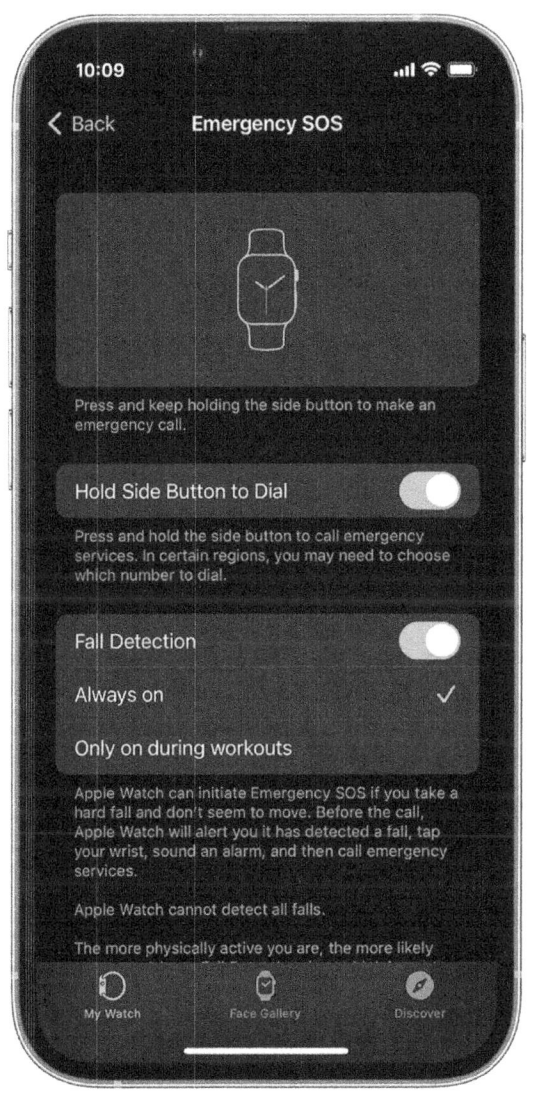

If you entered your age while setting up your watch, or in the Health application, and you are age 55 & above, the fall detection feature would be activated automatically. Ensure that your correct age is reflected in your Medical ID and health information. Fall Detection is only available for 18 years or older.

Setup your Medical ID and add emergency contacts

- Enter the settings application on your Phone, touch **Health**, then click on **Medical ID**.
- Click on the **Edit** button.
- Fill in your date of birth and other health info.
- To add an emergency contact, click the add icon ![add icon], in the emergency contacts section. Click on a contact and enter their relationship.
- To delete an emergency contact from the list, click the remove icon ![remove icon] beside the contact, and touch the Delete button.
- To make your health more accessible from the lock screen, activate **Show when locked**. This would provide information in an emergency to people who want to help. Activate **Share During Emergency Call** to share your Medical info with paramedics. When you call or send an SMS to emergency services on your Phone or

Watch, your medical ID will be automatically shared with them
❖ Click the Done button.

You cannot set up emergency services as an emergency contact.

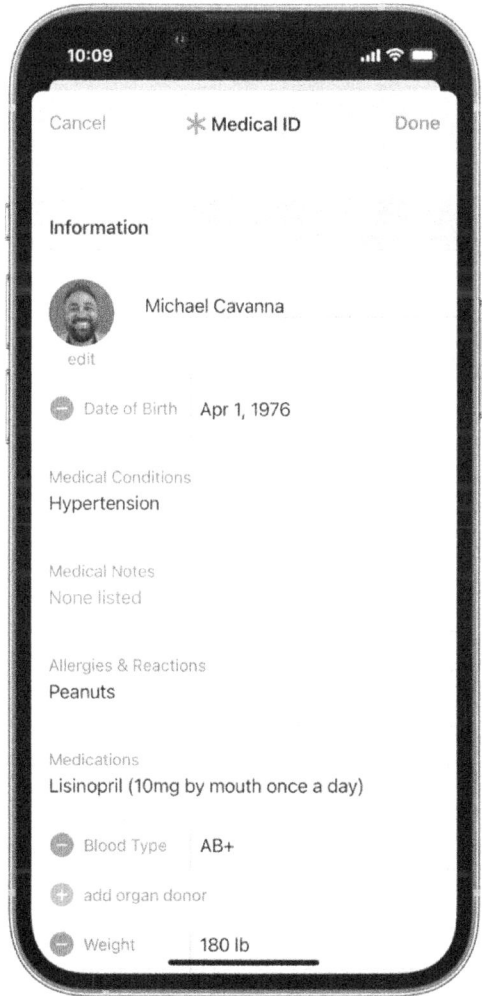

HANDWASHING FEATURE

The Apple Watch can detect when you start washing and will ask you to continue for 20 seconds which is the time recommended by the Global Health Organization. If you have not washed your hands within a few minutes of returning home, the Apple Watch notify you to let you know.

Activate hand washing

❖ Enter the Settings application on your Apple Watch.

❖ Touch the Handwashing button, then activate the Hand-washing timer.

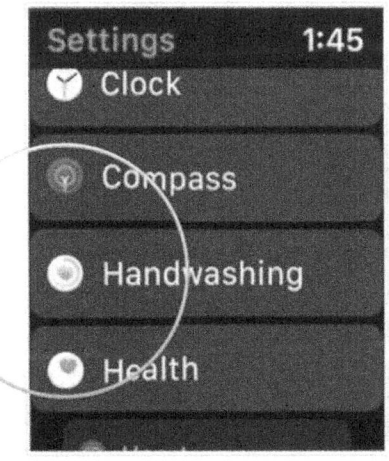 

If the Apple Watch detects that you have started washing your hands, it will start a 20-sec timer. If you stop washing for less than 20 seconds, it would encourage you to continue washing.

Get hand washing notifications

The Apple Watch can remind you to wash your hands after you get home.

❖ Enter the Settings application on your Watch.
❖ Touch Handwashing, then activate Handwashing Reminder.

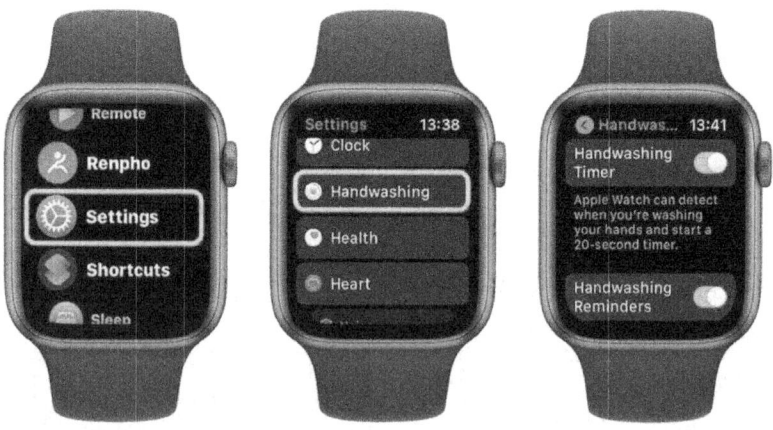

If you want to get handwashing reminders, you need to enter a home address in your My Card in the Contacts application on your Phone.

To view a report on the average hand-washing time, enter the Health application on your Phone, head over to Browse > Other Data, and click on the Hand-washing button.

ACTIVITY APP

The Activity application on the Apple Watch monitors your activity throughout the day and encourages you to reach your fitness goals. The application monitors how often you stand, how much you move, and how many minutes you exercise. 3 rings in different colours sum up your progress. The target is to sit less, move more, and exercise by filling each ring every day.

The Fitness application on your iPhone records your activity. If you have tracked about 6 months of activity, it shows daily trend data for flight climbed, walk distance, minutes of standing, hours of standing, minutes of exercise, active calories, and so on. In the Fitness application on your Phone, click on Summary and go to Trends to see how you're doing compared to your regular activity.

Get started

When setting up your Watch, you are asked if you want to configure the Activity application. If you did not, you can do so the first time you launch the Activity application.

❖ Launch the Activity application on your Watch.
❖ Swipe to the left to read the Stand, Exercise, & Move descriptions, then touch the Get Started button.
❖ Utilize the Digital Crown to choose your gender, weight, height, age, & whether you use a wheelchair.
❖ Pick an activity level & start to move.

Check your progress

Enter the Activity application on your watch at any time to view your progress. The Activity application would show 3 rings.

- ❖ The blue Stand ring displays how many times you stand & move for at least 1 minute per hour in a day.
- ❖ The green Exercise ring displays how many minutes of brisk activity you have done.
- ❖ The red Move ring displays how many active calories you have burned.

If you are using a wheelchair, the blue Standing ring turns into a Rotating ring, showing how many times you have rolled for a minimum of a minute per hour in a day.

Rotate the Digital Crown to see your present totals – continue to scroll to see your progress in graphical form, your overall steps, workout, total distance, & flight.

When a ring overlaps, it means you have passed your goal. Rotate the Digital Crown, then click on the Weekly Summary to see the week's progress.

Check your weekly summary

- ❖ Launch the Activity application on your watch.
- ❖ Rotate the digital crown to navigate to the bottom of your display, and click on **weekly summary**.

Change your goals

If you think your activity goals are too complex or not difficult, you can change them.

❖ Launch the Activity application on your watch.
❖ Rotate the Digital Crown to navigate to the bottom of your display, and click the **Change Goals** button.
❖ Click the Minus button or the Add button to make changes to a goal, and then click on Next.

Every Monday, you will receive a notification about the achievements of the previous week and you can set your goals for the next week.

View your activity history

❖ Enter the Fitness application on your Phone, and click the Summary button.
❖ Touch the Activity field, click the Calendar button , and then touch a date.

View your trends

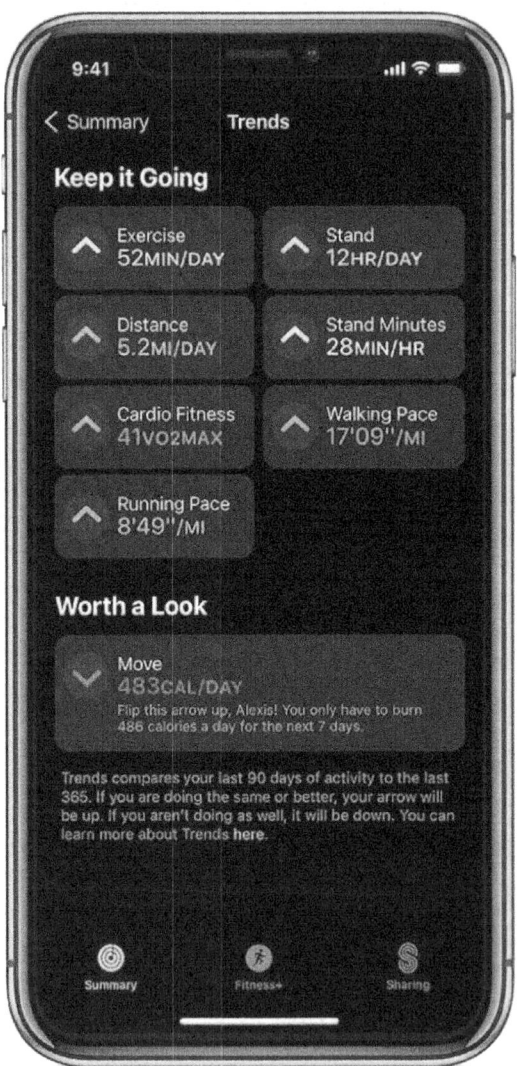

In the Fitness application on your Phone, the Trends area displays daily trend information for active calories, exercise minutes, standing hours, standing minutes, walking distance & cardio fitness. It compares your last 90 days of activity to the last 365.

To see how you're doing, adhere to the directives below:

- Launch the Fitness application on your Phone, and click on the Summary button.
- Swipe up to see trends.
- Touch **See more** if you want to know how to turn a trend.
- Click on a trend to its history.

If a metric's trend arrow points up, you are maintaining or improving your level of fitness. If the arrow faces down, your 90-day average for that metric has begun to decline.

View your awards

You can receive awards for streaks, personal records, & major milestones using

your watch. To check out your awards adhere to the directives below:

- Enter the Activity application on your watch.

- ❖ Swipe to the left 2 times to go to your awards screen.
- ❖ Scroll up to view your awards. Touch an award to see more info about it.

You can also launch the Fitness application on your Phone, click on the Summary button, and swipe up to view Awards at the bottom of your display.

Control activity reminders

Reminders can help you reach your goals. The Apple Watch would tell you if you are on track or falling behind the goals you set. Adhere to these guidelines to select the reminders & alerts you want to see:

- ❖ Enter the Settings application on your Watch.
- ❖ Touch Activity, and configure the notifications.

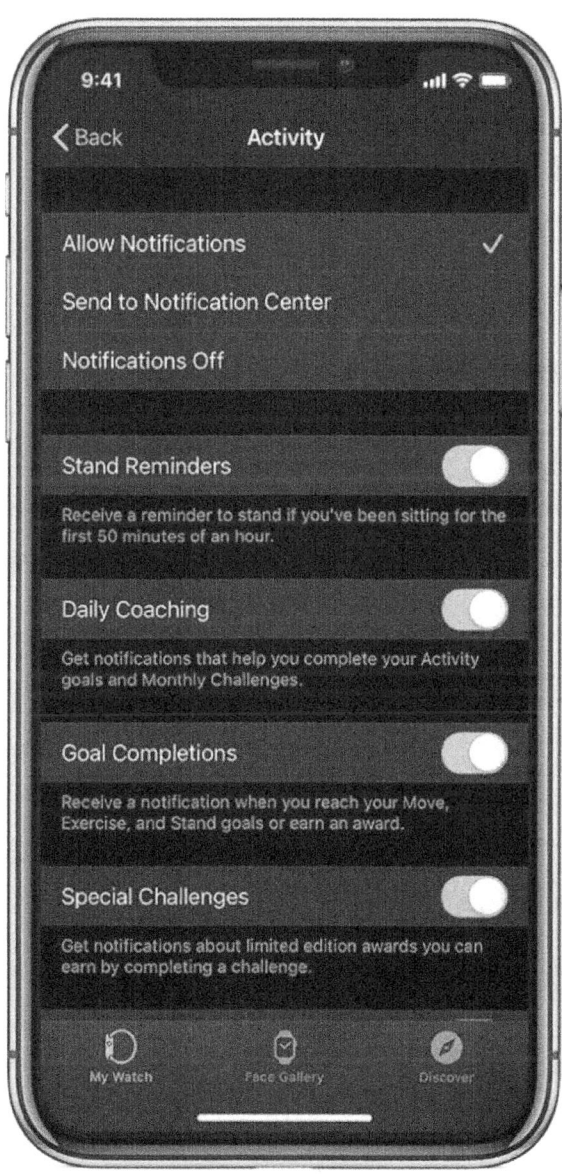

Suspend daily coaching

To deactivate activity reminders, adhere to the guidelines below:

❖ Enter the Watch application on your Phone and touch My Watch.
❖ Click on Activity, then deactivate Daily Coaching.

Share your activity

You can share your activity with loved ones — you can also share them with a coach or trainer. You can receive alerts when your friends reach their goals, complete exercises, and get achievements.

Add or remove a friend

If you haven't shared activity before, launch the Fitness application on your Phone, and click on Sharing. Click on **Get Started**, and adhere to the directives below:

- Launch the Activity application on your Watch.
- Swipe to the left, then rotate the Digital Crown to go to the bottom of your display.
- To add a friend, touch **Invite a Friend**, and then click on a Friend.

To remove a friend, click a friend you are sharing with, and then click on Remove.

After your invitation has been accepted by your friend, you can see his or her activity and he or she can see yours. If a friend has not accepted your invitation, click their name in the Invited segment of the Share screen, and then click on **Invite Again**.

To add a friend, you can also enter the Fitness application on your Phone, click on Sharing, click the **Invite a friend** button, and click the Plus button to send an email invitation, or click the Message button to send an invitation with the Message app.

View the progress of your friends

- Launch the Activity application on your Watch.
- Swipe to the left, then rotate the Digital Crown to go to your friends' list.
- Touch Friends to see statistics for the day.

Compete with your friends

You can invite your friends to a 7-day competition. During the competition, you will each receive points for filling your rings. You will receive one point for every percentage you add to your ring per day and you can get up to 600 points per day. The person with the highest score at the end of the competition wins. During the competition, a notification tells you if you are ahead or behind your competitor.

- Launch the Activity application on your Watch.
- Swipe to the left, click on a Friend, and click on **Compete**.
- Click on Invite, and wait for your friend to accept.

Or, when you get an Activity sharing alert — your friend has closed their ring or doubled their move goal, for example — you can scroll down and touch **Compete**.

You can also launch the Fitness application on your Phone, touch Sharing, touch a Friend, and click Compete with [the name of your friend].

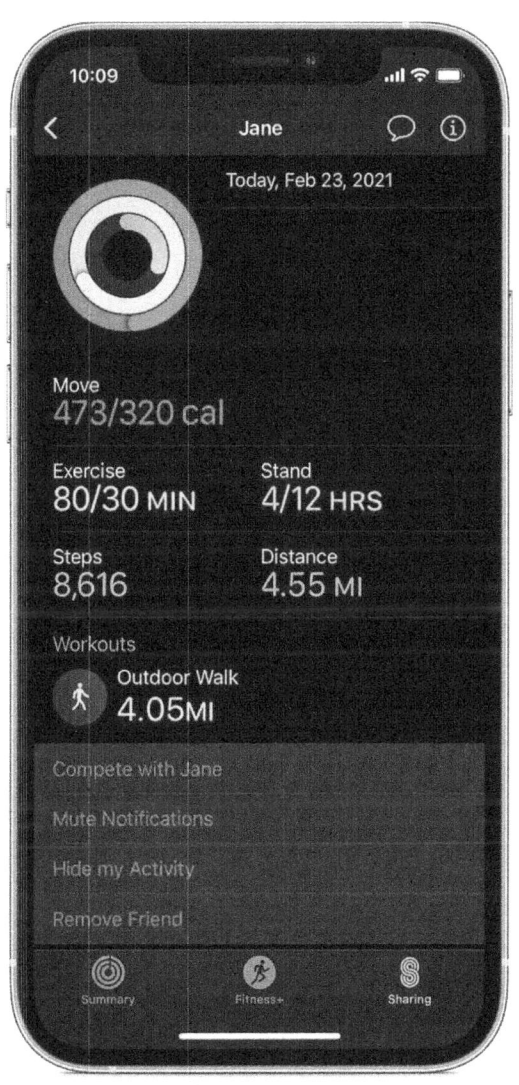

Adjust the friend settings

You can easily make changes to your friend settings. Simply launch the Activity application on your

Watch, swipe to the left, click on a friend, scroll down, then do any of the below:

❖ Silent Notifications for that friend: Touch Mute Notification.
❖ Hide your activity from that friend: Touch Hide my activity.
❖ Remove that Friend: Click Remove Friend.

MEASURE BLOOD OXYGEN LEVEL WITH YOUR WATCH

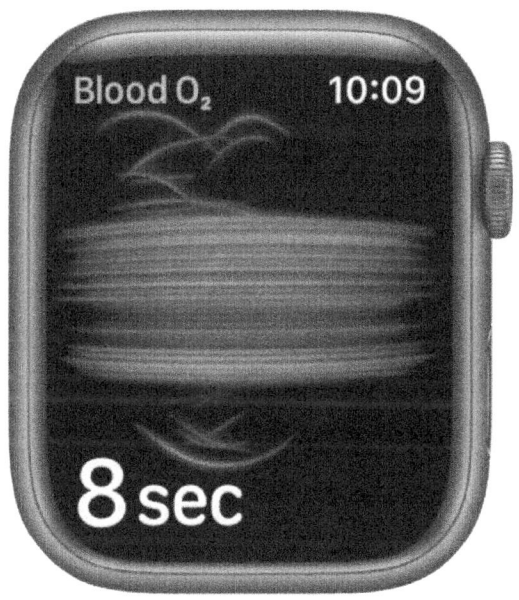

Use the Blood Oxygen application on your watch to measure the percentage of oxygen carried by red blood cells from the lungs to the body. Knowing the amount of oxygen in your blood can help you understand your health and your overall well-being.

Setup Blood Oxygen

❖ Enter the Settings application on your Watch.
❖ Touch Blood Oxygen, and activate Blood Oxygen measurement.

Deactivate background measurement in theater & sleep mode

Measurements of blood oxygen use a bright red light that shines on your wrist, which may be more visible in dark areas. You can deactivate measurement if the light is distracting you.

❖ Enter the Settings application on your Watch.
❖ Touch Blood Oxygen, then deactivate In Theatre Mode & In Sleep Mode.

Measure the oxygen level of your blood

The blood oxygen application , measure the level of oxygen in your blood occasionally during the day if you activate Background Measurement, but you can measure it whenever you want.

❖ Launch the Blood Oxygen application on your Watch.

❖ Place your hand on a table or on your lap, and ensure your wrist is flat, with your watch screen facing up.
❖ Touch the Start button, and hold your arm for 15 seconds.
❖ You will get the results when the measurement is complete. Touch Done.

Note: To get the best results, you need to allow the back of your watch to come in contact with your skin. Don't allow your watch to be too tight or too loose on your wrist, give the skin room to breath.

See the history of your blood oxygen measurements

❖ Enter the health application on your Phone.
❖ Touch the Browse button, touch Respiratory, and then touch Blood Oxygen.

COMPASS

The Compass application displays the direction your watch is facing, your location & elevation.

View your bearings, coordinates, incline, & elevation

Your bearing is displayed on the upper left. Rotate the Digital Crown to go up & view your incline, coordinates, & elevation.

- Launch the Compass application on your Watch.
- Hold the Apple Watch flat to get accurate bearings.
- To add a bearing, rotate the Digital Crown to go up, click on the **Add Bearing** button, turn your watch to the bearing, and touch Done.
  To adjust the bearings, rotate the Digital Crown to go up, click Edit Bearing, convert your Apple

Watch to the new bearings, and click the Done button.
- ❖ Rotate the Digital Crown to go up, touch Clear Bearing to clear the bearing.

Add the elevation complication to your watch face

The always-on altimeter, on your watch, allows you to monitor your elevation in real time. Add the elevation complication to the face of your watch to view your elevation easily.

- ❖ Long press your watch face display, then touch Edit.
- ❖ Swipe to the left till you get to the end.
- ❖ Click on a complication to choose it, rotate the Digital Crown to compass, and select Elevation.
- ❖ Click the Digital Crown to save the changes you have made, and touch the face to use it.

Note: If Location Service is disabled, Compass would note show coordinates or elevation. To activate or deactivate Location Services, enter the Settings application on your Watch, click on the Privacy button, and then click on Location Services.

To use True North, instead of magnetic north, enter the Settings application on your Watch, click on Compass, and activate Use True North.

SCHOOLTIME

The School-Time feature reduces the Apple Watch features during school hours, which allows a family member to focus.

Setup SchoolTime

- Enter the Watch application on the phone you are using to manage the watch.
- Click on **All Watches**, then touch the watch in the Family Watches section.
- Click on the Done button and click on School Time.
- Activate School-Time, then touch Edit Schedule.
- Select the days & times you want School Time to be active.
- Touch Add Time if you want to setup many schedules in a day, for instance from 8:00a.m. to noon, and then from 1:00p.m. to 3:00pm.

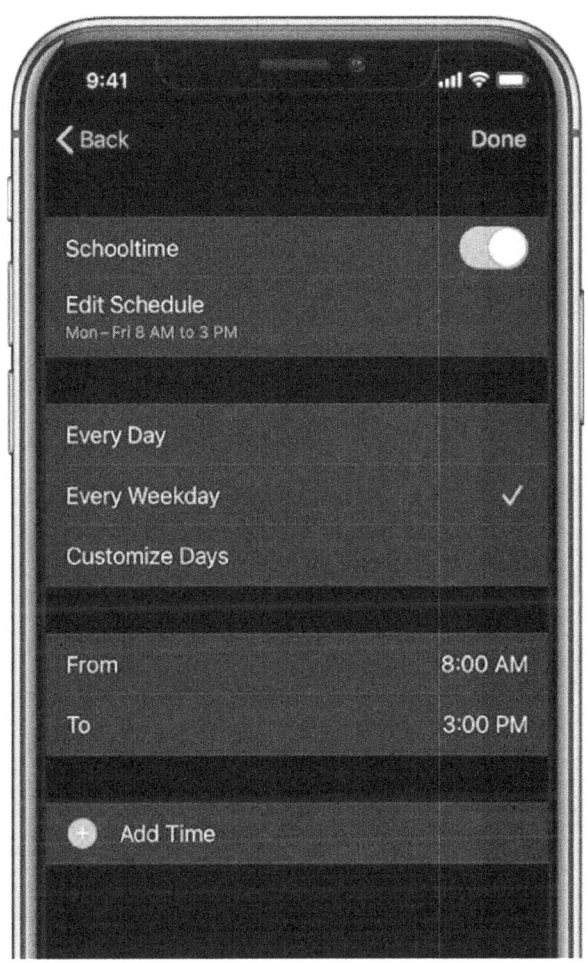

Leave School-Time

The person using the watch can exit School Time temporarily, maybe to check their activity rings.

Touch the screen, rotate the Digital Crown, and touch Exit.

If you leave School-Time during active hours, the School Time watch face would return when you put your hand down.

See when School Time was unlocked

When your family member leaves School Time, you will get a report on when and how long they left. To view the report, follow these steps:

- ❖ Launch the Watch application on the phone you are using to manage the watch.
- ❖ Touch All Watches, then touch the watch in the Family Watches section.
- ❖ Click on the Done button and click on School Time.
- ❖ Swipe up to see the report.

Tip: When School Time is not active, your family member can activate it. Simply open the Control Centre and tap the School time button. To leave School Time, simply rotate the Digital Time

CYCLE TRACKING

Use the Cycle Monitoring application to record information about your menstrual cycle. You can add flow info & record symptoms like cramps or headaches. With the info you enter, the Cycle Tracking application can notify you after predicting that your next fertile window or period is about to begin. The application can utilize the heart rate info on your Watch to improve prediction.

Setup Cycle Tracking

- Enter the Health application on your iPhone.
- Click the **Browse** button on the bottom right to show the health categories screen.
- Touch Cycle Tracking
- Click the **Get Started** button, and adhere to the directives on your display to setup notifications & other options.
- Touch Options, then activate the options you want – Fertility Prediction, Period Prediction, & Heart Rate Info.

How to track your cycle

❖ Launch the Health application on your Phone and click the **Browse** button.

- ❖ Touch Cycle Tracking.
- ❖ Go to the appropriate day by swiping then touch the oval to record your period.
- ❖ To add more info, scroll down and click on a category, make changes, and click the Done button. You can keep track of body temperature, spotting, symptoms, etc.

To monitor your cycle from your watch, launch the Cycle Tracking application, go to the correct date by swiping, and click the oval to record your period.

Add cycle factors

You can also add factors that can affect the duration and length of your cycle, such as pregnancy.

- ❖ Launch the Health application on your Phone and click the Browse button.
- ❖ Touch the Cycle Tracking button.
- ❖ In the Cycle Log segment, touch the Setup button beside Factors.
- ❖ Choose Using Contraceptives, Lactating, Pregnant, or None.

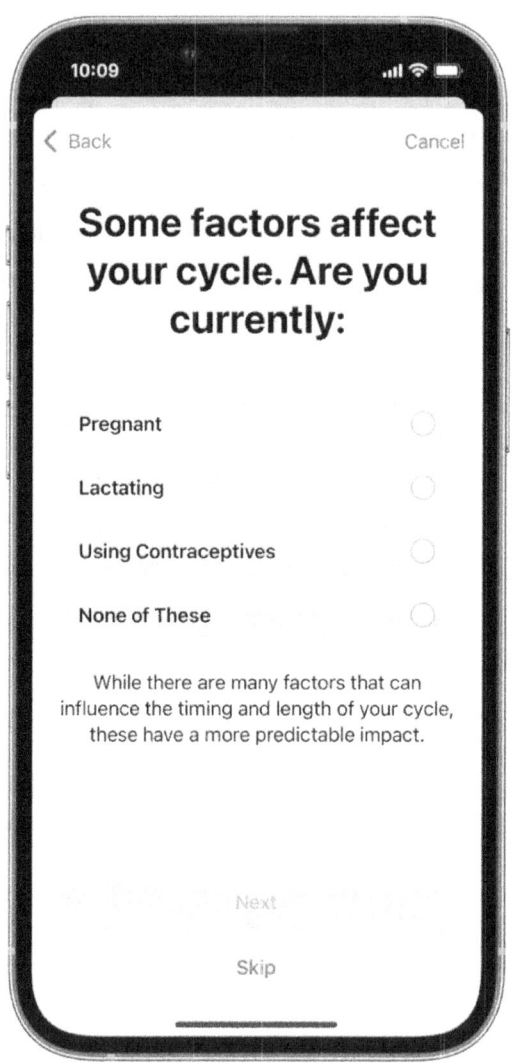

❖ Enter the Factor start date and click on the Done button.

If a factor is incorrectly added, click on the factor and click the Delete Factor button to erase it.

To end a factor, click on it, and touch Ended. Enter the end date and touch Done. You can click the **Show All Factors** button to view the history of your previous factors.

What the colours mean

When you enter the Health application or Cycle Tracking application, it is simple to view your fertile or period window. This is the meaning of the symbols and colors in the application.

The light blue colour symbolizes the predicted 6-day fertile window.

Circular red strides symbolize when your period is expected to happen.

●

Solid red circle symbolizes your recorded period days.

●

The purple dot indicates the days you entered your details.

Log your cycle on your watch

❖ Enter the Cycle Tracking application on your Watch.
❖ Touch the buttons & select the options that portray your period-for example your symptoms & flow level.

The information you provide would show in the Cycle log on your Phone.

How to check the date for your next & last period

To check the dates on your Watch, adhere to the guidelines below:

❖ Launch the Cycle Tracking application
❖ Scroll down to Last Menstrual Period or Period Prediction.

How to set fertility & period tracking notifications & prediction info

❖ Launch the Health application on your Phone and click the **Browse** button.

❖ Touch Cycle Tracking.
❖ Scroll down, and touch **Option**.

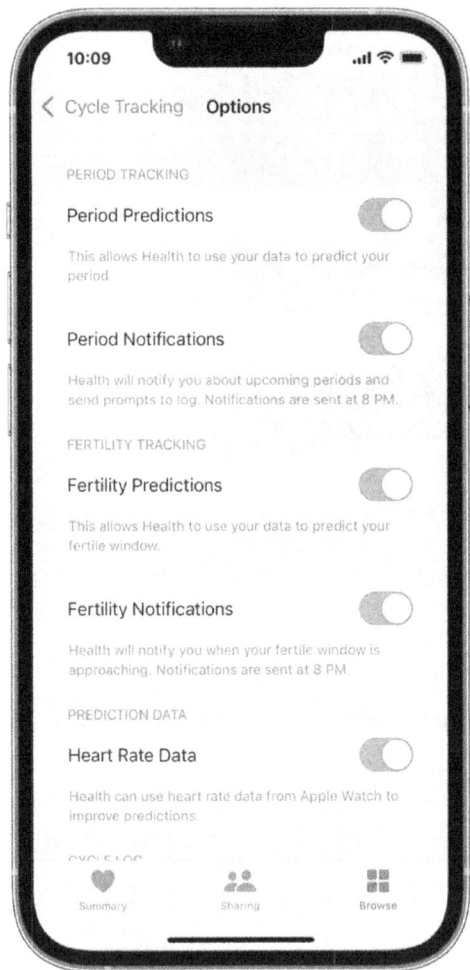

❖ Choose Period Notification & Period prediction. These notifications would allow you to know when your period starts.

❖ Choose Fertility Notification & Fertility Prediction. These notifications would allow you to know when your fertile window may begin.

The Predictions start after entering your last period in the Cycle Tracking application and are based on the recorded information. If you record a period before it is predicted to start, you would not receive a period forecast notification for that cycle.

How prediction is calculated

Period forecasts are based on the information you have entered about your previous cycle & period length, as well as the length of your normal cycle & the number of days your period lasts. After setting up Cycle Tracking, you can enter information about your cycle history, such as the date of the last period, the normal length, and the length of your normal cycle. Daily recording of your period helps to improve prediction calculations.

How to hide the cycle tracking application

You can remove applications from your watch's Home screen.

- Click the Digital Crown to view the home screen.
- Long-Press the Cycle Tracking application till the application icon starts jiggling. If the application does not start jiggling, ensure that you aren't pressing too hard
- Touch the Erase button ⊗ and click Delete application.
- Click the Digital Crown to finish.

If your applications are in List format, swipe to the left on the Cycle Tracking application and click the Trash icon to delete it.

PHONE & CONTACT APP

In the Contacts application , you can view, edit, & share contacts with other Apple devices that utilize the same Apple ID.

View contacts on your watch

❖ Launch the Contacts application on your Watch.

- ❖ Rotate the Digital Crown to go through your contacts.
- ❖ Touch a contact to see address info & notes.

If the contact has a profile picture, touch it to expand it.

Communicate with contacts

- ❖ Launch the Contacts application on your Watch.
- ❖ Rotate the Digital Crown to go through your contacts.
- ❖ Click a contact, and do any of the below:

➢ Touch the phone icon to view the phone number of the contact. Touch a phone number to call.
➢ Click the Message icon to open a message thread or start a new one.
➢ Click the E-mail icon to create an e-mail message.
➢ To invite someone to a Walkie-Talkie, press the Walkie-Talkie button , or if they have already accepted your invitation and Walkie-Talkie is activated, start a Walkie-Talkie conversation.

Create a contact

❖ Enter the Contacts application on your Watch.
❖ Click the New Contact button at the top of your display.
❖ Enter the name of the contact and company if necessary.
❖ Add an e-mail, phone number, & address, and touch Done.

Share, edit, or delete contacts

- Launch the Contacts application on your watch.
- Rotate the Digital Crown to go through your contacts.
- Click on a contact, go down, and then click Delete, Edit, or Share Contact.

Make a call

- Launch the Phone application on your Watch.
- Touch **Contacts** and rotate the Digital Crown to go down.
- Click the contact you want to call and press the call icon.
- Touch FaceTime Audio to make a voice call with Face-Time or touch a number.
- Rotate the Digital Crown to adjust the volume while on a call.

Tip: To call someone you recently spoke to, click the "Recent" button and then touch the contact.

Enter a phone number

- Enter the Phone application on your watch.
- Touch Keypad, enter the number and touch the Call key .

You can also utilize the keypad to enter additional numbers while a call. Just touch the More button and touch the Keypad button.

View call details

If you are talking on your phone, you can view your call details on your Watch in the Phone application. You can also end a call from your watch (for example, if you are making use of a headset or earphones).

Answer a call

When you get a call alert, lift your hand to see who is calling.

- Send the call to voicemail: Touch the red Reject button in the incoming call alert.
- Answer calls on your watch: Touch the answer key to speak with the inbuilt microphone &

speaker or a Bluetooth device connected with your watch.
- ❖ Answer with your Phone or send an SMS instead: Click the More button ••• and click on an option. When you touch the Answer button on your phone, the call would be placed on hold and the person calling will hear a repetitive tone till you answer with the paired Phone.

If you cannot find your iPhone, long-press the bottom of your display, swipe up, and touch the Ping iPhone button 📳 on your watch.

While on a call

If you are on a call that does not utilize Face-Time audio, you can transfer calls to your iPhone, increase or reduce the ringtone, enter numbers through the keyboard, and transfer calls to other audio devices.

❖ Move a call from your watch to your Phone: while speaking on your watch, open your Phone and click the green button or line at the upper part of your display.

❖ Adjust call volume: Rotate the Digital Crown. Touch the mute button 🎤 to mute yourself (for example, if you are on a conference call).
❖ Enter number while on a call: Touch the More button ●●●, touch Keypad, and press the number.
❖ Move the call to an audio device: Touch the more button ●●●, then select the device.

While on a Face-Time voice call, you can increase or reduce the volume, silent the call by touching the Silent button 🎤, or touch the More button ●●● and select an audio destination.

Listen to voicemail

If the caller leaves a voice mail, you will receive a message - click on the "Play" button in the notification to play it. To listen to it some other time, enter the Phone application on your Watch and click Voicemail.

ECG

An electrocardiogram (also called an ECG or ECG) is a test that records the intensity & timing of electrical signals that cause a heartbeat. By checking the ECG, your doctor can get an idea of your heart rate and look for abnormalities.

How to use the ECG application

The ECG application can record your rhythm & heart beat with your watch's electric heart sensor, and then record (AFib).

The ECG application would record an electrocardiogram showing the electrical pulse that makes your heart-beat. The ECG application monitors these heartbeats to get the heart rate and determine if your heart's lower & upper chambers are in rhythm. If they are out of rhythm, it could be Atrial Fibrillation.

Install & setup the ECG application

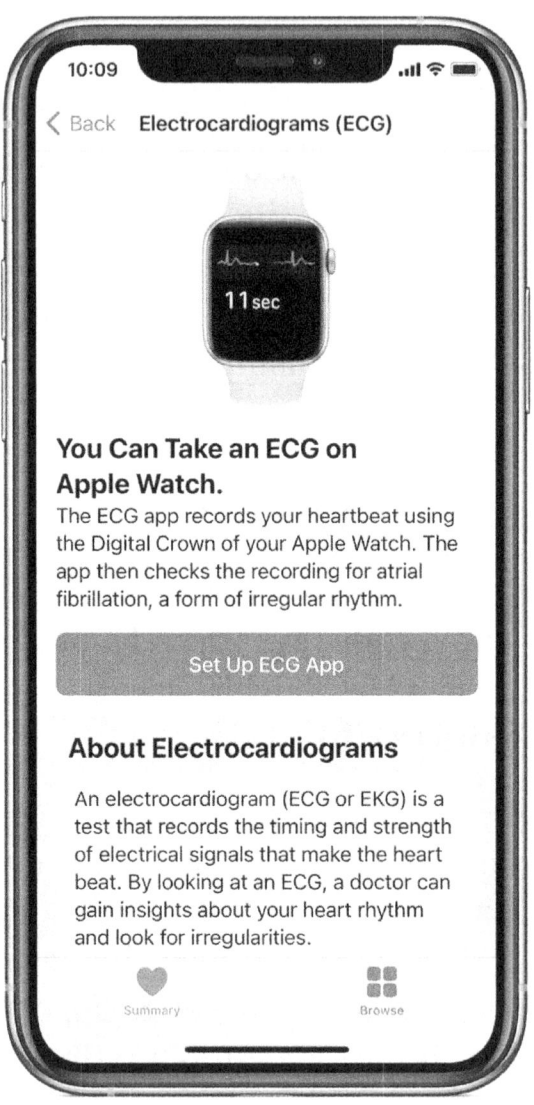

The ECG application is installed when you set it up in the Health application. Adhere to the directives below to setup the ECG application:

❖ Enter the Health application on your Phone.
❖ Adhere to the steps on your screen. If you do not see the setup prompt, touch the "Browse" button, and touch Heart> Electrocardiogram (ECG)> Setup ECG Application.
❖ After setting up the ECG application, launch the ECG application to get an ECG.

If you still cannot find the application on your watch, launch the Watch application on your Phone and touch the **Heart** button. In the ECG segment, touch the Install button to install the ECG application.

Note: The ECG application is not intended for use by persons under 22 years of age.

Perform an ECG

At any time, you can take an ECG when you experience symptoms such as a skipped or fast heartbeat, when you have other heart health issues, or when you receive an abnormal rhythm message.

❖ Ensure your Watch is snug & on the hand you choose in the Watch application. To verify, launch the Watch application, click on My

Watch, and head over to General> Watch Orientation.

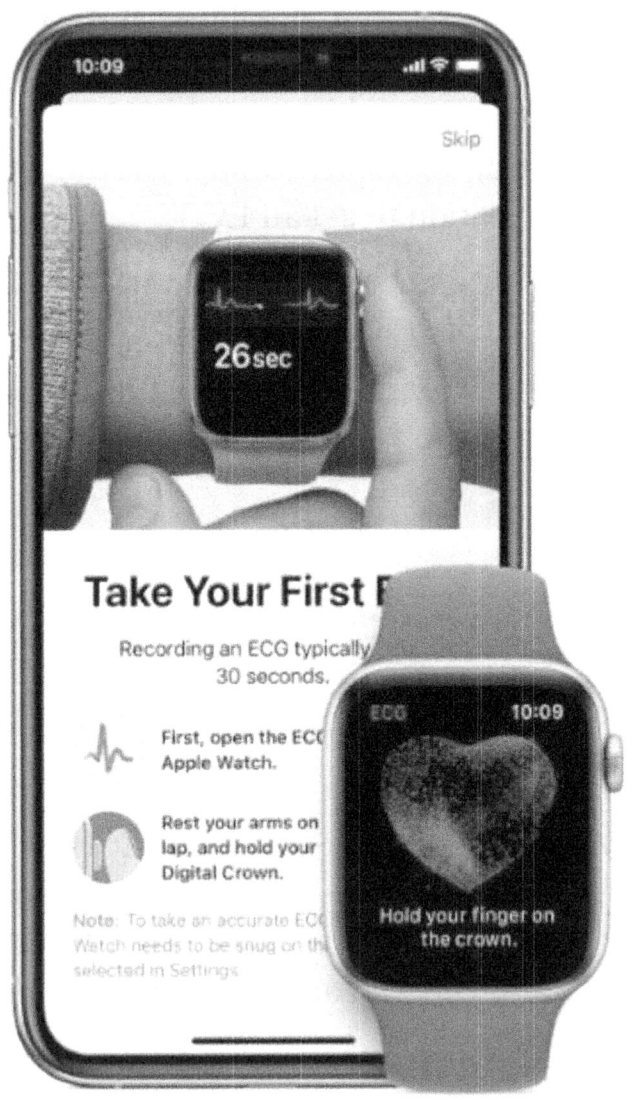

- ❖ Launch the ECG application on your Watch.
- ❖ Put your hands on a table or on your lap.

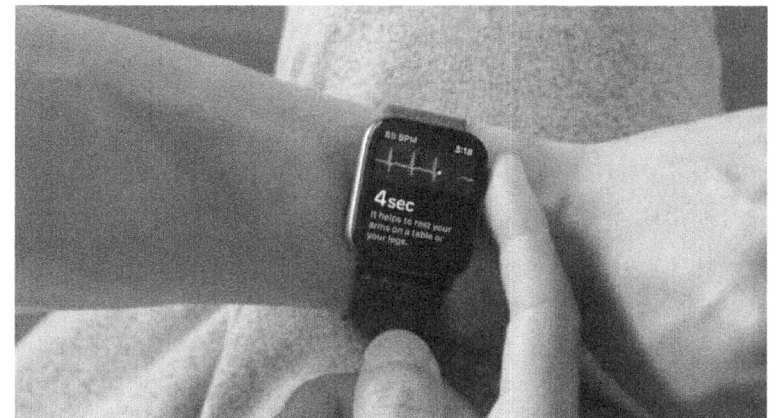

❖ Hold your finger on the Digital Crown. There is no need to press the Digital Crown while taking an ECG.

❖ Wait. It takes 30 seconds to complete a session. Once the recording is complete you will get a classification, you can touch the Add Symptoms button and choose your symptoms.
❖ Click the Save button to note Symptoms, and you're done.

How to read the results

After taking an ECG, you would get the following results on the ECG application. Regardless of what the result says, if you are not feeling fine or have any symptoms, you should see your doctor.

Sinus rhythm

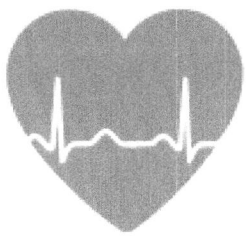

The effect of sinus rhythm means that the heart beats uniformly between 50 & 100 BPM. This occurs when the lower & upper chambers of the heart synchronize in beating. The result applies only to that particular session & does not mean that your heart beats uniformly every time. Nor does it mean that you are healthy.

AFib

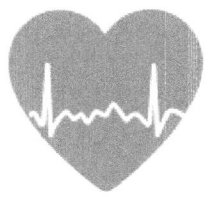

An Atrial fibrillation result implies that the heart is beating abnormally. AFib is the most common form of arrhythmia or heart palpitations. If you get an AFib classification and do not have an AFib diagnosis, you should see a doctor.

Low or high heart rate

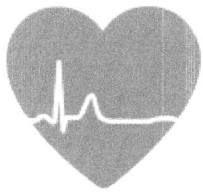

A heart-rate below 50BPM or above 120BPM affects in ECG version 1 would affect the ECG application's ability to detect AFib. In version 2 of the ECG, a heart-rate below 50 BPM or above 150 BPM may affect the ECG's application's ability to detect AFib.

Inconclusive

An inconclusive result implies that the session cannot be classified

View & share information about your health

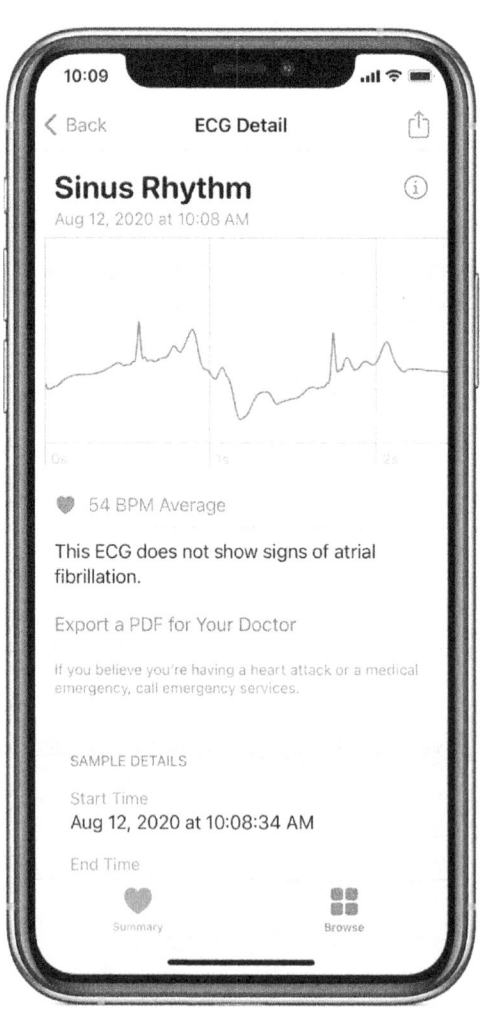

ECG wave form, associated classifications, and marked features will be stored in the Health application on your Phone. You can also share a PDF with your doctor.

- Launch the health application.
- Touch the Browse tab, touch Heart> Electrocardiogram (ECG).
- Click on the chart to see your ECG results.
- Click on the Export PDF for your Doctor.
- Click the Share button to share or print the PDF.

How to get the best results

- Place your hands on your lap or on a table. Try to relax and don't move too much.
- Ensure your watch isn't slung around your wrist. The back of the Apple Watch should touch your skin.
- Ensure your wrist & your watch are dry & clean
- Ensure your watch is on the hand you choose in the Watch application.
- To avoid electronic interference, avoid all electronic devices that are plugged to an outlet

HEART RATE APP

Your heart rate is a great way to monitor your health. You can check your heart rate while working out; checkout your rest, gait, breathing, exercise walking, & recovery rates all through the day; or check it out whenever you want.

View your heart rate

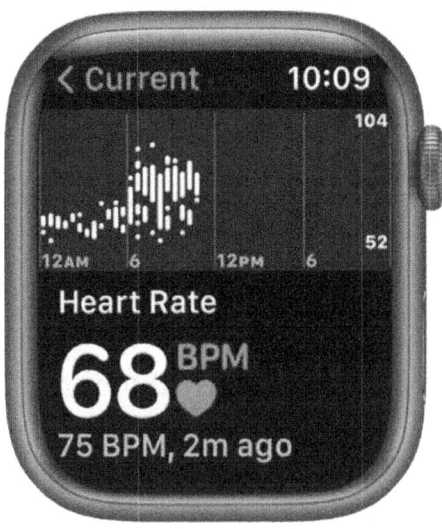

Launch the heart rate application on your watch to see your current heart-rate, resting rate, and average walking rate.

Your watch would continue to measure your heart rate as long as you are putting it on.

Check your heart rate while working out

Generally, your heart rate is shown on the multiple metric workout display. Adhere to the guidelines below to personalize the metrics that show when you are working out:

❖ Launch the watch application on your Phone.
❖ Click on My Watch, head over to Workout>Workout View, and then click on an Exercise.

See your heart rate data chart

- Launch the Health application on your Phone.
- Touch **Browse** at the lower right, touch Heart, and tap Heart-rate.
- Swipe up to add a heart rate to your summary, and then click the Add to Favorites button.

Get low or high heart rate notifications

After a minimum of 10 minutes of inactivity, the Apple Watch can notify you if your heart rate is below or above a selected threshold. You can activate the heart rate alert the first time you launch the Heart rate application, or at any time thereafter.

- Launch your watch's Settings application, and click on the Heart button.
- Click the Low Heart Rate Notification or High Heart Rate Notification, then enter your heart rate threshold.

You can also launch the Watch application on your Phone, touch My Watch, then touch Heart. Ouch Low heart rate or High heart rate, and set a threshold.

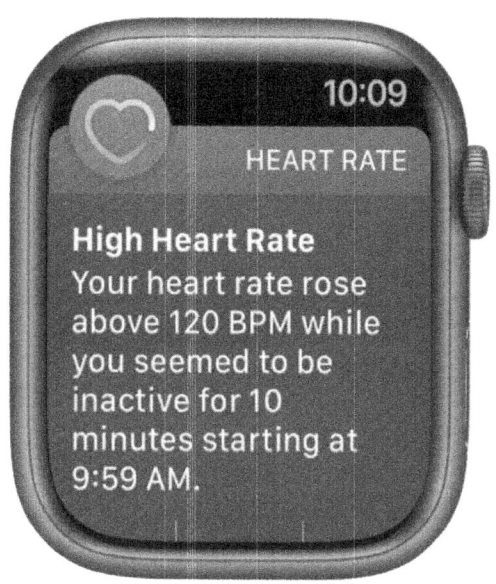

Get irregular heart rhythm alerts

You can get a message if your watch detects an irregular heart rhythm that could be atrial fibrillation (AFib).

❖ Enter your watch's Settings application.
❖ Touch Heart, then activate Irregular Rhythm Notification.

You can also launch the Watch application on your Phone, click on My Watch, click Heart, and activate Irregular Rhythm.

MAIL

Select which mail-box appears on your Watch

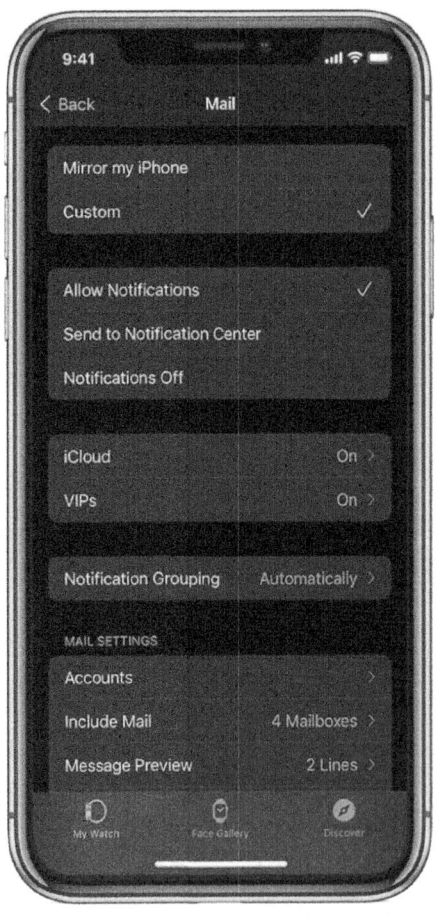

- ❖ Enter the Watch application on your Phone.
- ❖ Click on My Watch, then head over to Mail> Include Mail.

- Click on the account you want to see in the Accounts section of your Watch.
- If you want, click on an account and click on a specific mailbox to see what's inside the mailbox on your watch.

Read the emails in the mail application

- Launch your watch's Mail application ⭕.
- Rotate the Digital Crown to scroll through the message catalog.
- Click on a message to read it.
- To go to the beginning of a long message, rotate the Digital Crown or tap the top of your display.

Switch to your iPhone

When you get an email you want to read on your Phone, adhere to the guidelines below:

❖ Open your iPhone.
❖ On a Face ID iPhone, swipe up from the bottom edge of your screen & stop to reveal the Application Switcher. (On iPhones with a Home button, double-click the Home button to display the Application Switcher.)

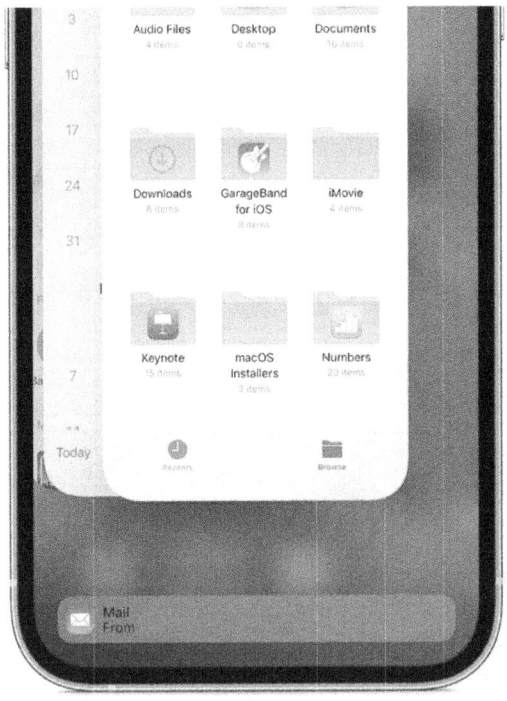

❖ Touch the button at the lower part of your display to open the mail.

Create a message

❖ Enter the watch's Mail application.
❖ Utilize the Digital Crown to go to the top of your display, and click New Message.
❖ Click on Add Contact to add a recipient, click Add Subject to create a subject line, and then click Create Message.

If you have setup your watch to utilize more than one language, click Languages, select a language, and then click the Create Message field.

Compose a message

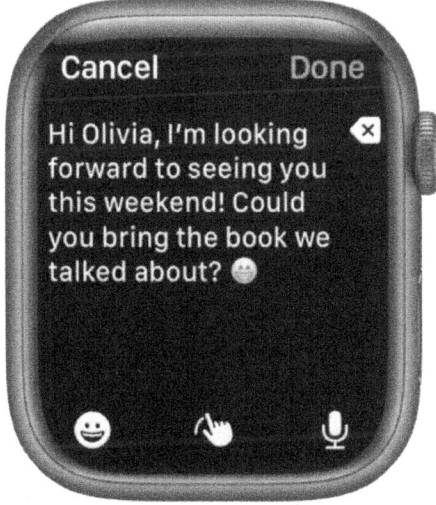

Your message can be composed in many ways - mainly on one screen. Click on the Create message field & do any or a combination of the below:

- ❖ Utilize the QuickPath & QWERTY keyboards to finish a word.
  If you do not see the keyboard, swipe up from the bottom part of your screen, then touch the Keyboard button.
- ❖ Utilize Scribble: Utilize your fingers to write what you want. To edit what you are writing, rotate the Digital Crown to put the cursor where you want, and then make corrections.
- ❖ Dictate: Touch the Dictate button 🎤, say what you want, and touch the Done button. You can also say the punctuation mark as well- for instance, "have you seen it question mark"
  To go back to making use of Scribble, rotate the Digital Crown or touch the Scribble button ✋.
- ❖ Add an emoji: Click the emoji button ☺, click on the most frequently used emoji or category, and scroll to see the available images. When you see the relevant icon, click on it to add it to your message.
- ❖ Type with your Phone: When you start writing a message and if your paired iPhone is close, a notification will appear on your Phone suggesting

you enter text via the iOS keyboard. Touch the notification, and then type what you want using your phone's keyboard.

MEMOJI

With the Memoji application , you can create your own Memoji - you can choose skin tones, hairstyles & colours, facial expressions, hats, glasses, etc. You can create a lot of Memoji for different moods.

Create Memoji

❖ Enter the Memoji application on your watch.
❖ If you are making use of the Memoji application for the first time, click on the Get Started button.

If you have made a Memoji before, scroll up and click the Add memoji button⊕ to add another one.
- ❖ Click on each feature & scroll your watch's Digital Crown to select the option you want for the Memoji. If you add features like hairstyles & glasses, your character will come to life.
- ❖ Click on the Done button to add the memoji to your collection.

To create more Memoji, click the Add button⊕ and create the memoji.

Edit a Memoji, Create a Memoji watch face, and more

On your Watch, launch the Memoji application, click on a Memoji, and select an option:

- ❖ Edit a Memoji: Click on features like eyes & head wear, and rotate the Digital Crown to select a change.
- ❖ Create a memoji watch face: Scroll, and click on Create Watch Face.
  Go back to the watch face and swipe to the left to check out the new Memoji watch face.
- ❖ Duplicate any Memoji: Scroll, and click on Duplicate.
- ❖ Delete Memoji: Scroll and touch the Delete button.

MINDFULNESS

The Mindfulness application on your Watch recommends taking a few minutes each day to focus, concentrate & connect while you breathe. With an Apple Fitness +subscription, you can listen to Meditations live on your watch.

Start a meditation or breathing session

Launch the Mindfulness application on your watch, and do any of the below:

❖ Meditate: Click on the Reflect button, read the topic, focus, and click the Start button.

❖ Breath: Touch Breath, inhale slowly as the animation increases, and exhale as it decreases.

Swipe to the right to end before the session ends, and click the End button.

Set the duration of a session

❖ Launch the Mindfulness application on your Watch.
❖ Click the More Options button •••, click on Duration, and then select the duration.
❖ You can choose a time from 1 minute to 5 minutes.

Adjust the mindfulness settings

You can change how often you receive mindfulness reminders, silent reminders for the day, adjust the speed of your breathing and choose haptics settings.

Launch your watch's Settings application, click on Mindfulness, and do any of the below:

- Set reminders for mindfulness: In the Reminders segment, activate or deactivate Start of Day & End of Day; Click on the Add Reminder button to create more reminders.
- Receive or stop weekly summaries: activate or disable weekly summaries.
- Silent mindfulness reminder: Activate **Mute for today**.
- Adjust your breathing rate: Touch **Breathe Rate** to make changes to the number of breaths per minute.
- Select the haptics format: Touch Haptics, and select Prominent, Minimum, or None.
- Receive new meditations: Activate **Add New Meditation to Watch** so that your device can download new meditations once it's connected to power. Your finished meditations are automatically erased.

You can also launch the Watch application on your Phone, click on **My Watch**, click on **Mindfulness**, and make changes to the settings.

Make use of the Breath watch face

You can add the breath watch face for easy access to mindfulness sessions.

- ❖ With your present watch face showing, long-press your screen.
- ❖ Swipe to the left till you get to the end, then touch the New (+) button.
- ❖ Rotate the Digital Crown to choose Breath, and click the Add button.
- ❖ Click on the watch face to launch the Mindfulness application.

Begin a guided meditation

If you sign up for Apple Fitness +, you can listen to guided Meditations on your watch when you pair it with Airpods or other Bluetooth speakers.

- Enter the Mindfulness application on your watch.
- Touch Fitness + Audio Meditation.
- Go through the meditations by scrolling.
  The topics of meditation, coach, and length are close to the bottom of every episode
- Click on the Info button ⓘ to get more details about the Meditation, add it to your library, or play the meditation's as a playlist in the Music application.
- Click on a Meditation to start.

While the Meditation is playing, your present heart rate appears on your watch.

To stop or pause a guided meditation, swipe to the right while the meditation is playing, and then touch the Pause or End button. To start a workout while playing the meditation, click Workout, and select an exercise.

View Meditations you have completed

When you've done most or all of a Meditation, it will appear in My Library, which can be found on your watch.

- Enter the Mindfulness application on your watch.
- Touch Fitness + Audio Meditation.
- Go to the bottom of your display, and then click on My Library to display your Meditations.
- Click the Info button ⓘ to get more information about the Meditation, add it to your library, or play in the Music application.
- Click on a Meditation to play it once more.

NOISE

The Noise application 🎵 on your watch helps to measure the sound level around you through the microphone and the exposure duration. After detecting an increase in decibel level to the point that your hearing could get affected, your watch can notify you by tapping your wrist.

Note: The Noise application makes use of the Mic to measure and gauge the level of sound in your surroundings. The Apple Watch does not save or record any sound to measure these levels.

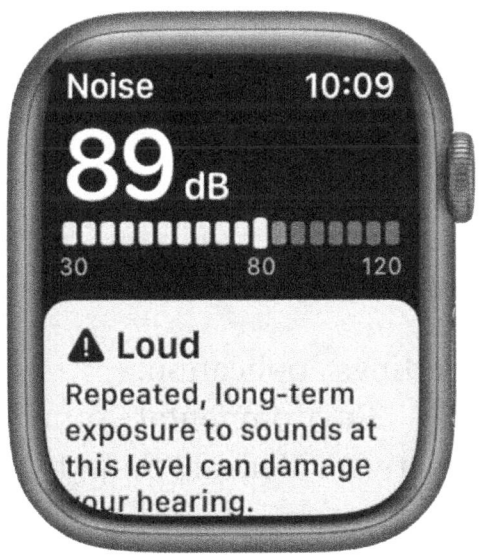

Setup the Noise application

- Launch the Noise application on your watch.
- Click on the Enable button to activate monitoring.
- In the future, open the Noise application or utilize the Noise complication to measure the sound around you.

Receive noise alerts

- Launch the Settings application on your watch.
- Head over to Noise> Noise Notification, and select any setting.

You can also launch the Watch application on your Phone, touch My Watch, then head over to Noise and click on Noise Threshold.

Deactivate noise measuring

- Launch your watch's Settings application.
- Head over to Noise> Environmental sound Measurement, then deactivate Measure Sound.

See the details of a noise notification

You can get messages from your watch on your phone when the sound in your environment gets to a certain level that may affect your ears.

To see the details of the notification, adhere to the directives below:

❖ Launch the Health application on your Phone and click on Summary on the bottom left.
❖ Click on the notification at the upper part of your display and click on More Details.

Checkout your exposure to the ambient sound levels over time

❖ Launch the Health application on your Phone, click on Browse, and then click on Hearing.
❖ Touch Environmental Sound Level, and do any of the below:
  ➢ Check the level of exposure over a certain period of time: Click on the tabs at the upper part of your display. (Levels are measured in decibels.)
  ➢ Get more info about the classification of sound level: Click the Info button ⓘ.
  ➢ Change the time frame shown on the graph: swipe the graph to the right or left.

CONTROL YOUR APPLE TV WITH YOUR WATCH

Your watch can be used as a remote control for any Apple TV when connected to the same Wi-Fi network.

Connect your Watch to Apple TV

If your iPhone is not connected to the WiFi network that your Apple TV is on before, join it now, then adhere to the directives below:

- Launch the Remote application ⏵ on your watch.
- Touch your Apple TV. If you do not see it, touch Add Device.
- On your Apple TV, head over to the Settings application> Remote & Devices> Remote Application & Device, then choose Apple Watch.
- Enter the code shown on your watch.

When the pairing icon shows beside appears Apple Watch, the watch is ready to control your TV.

Control your Apple Tv with your watch

Ensure your TV is awake, and adhere to the directives below:

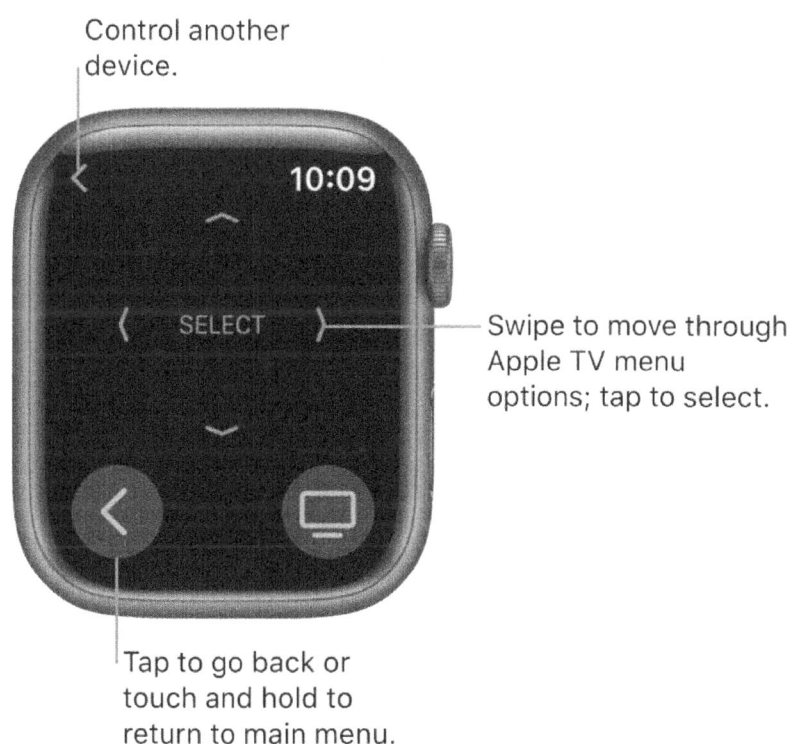

❖ Launch the Remote application on your watch.
❖ Select your Apple TV, then swipe right, left, down, or up, to navigate through the Apple TV menu options.
❖ Touch to select the selected item.

- Touch the Pause/Play button to resume or pause what is playing.
- Touch the Menu button to go back, or long-press it to go to the main menu.

Disconnect & remove the Apple TV

- On your TV, head over to the Settings application> Remote & Device> Remote Application & Device.
- Click on your Watch under Remote Application, and click on Unpair Device.
- Launch the Remote application on your watch and click the Remove button when the "lost connection" message shows up.

SLEEP APP

With the Sleep application , you can create a sleep schedule to reach your sleep goals. Put on your watch to sleep and the Apple Watch can monitor your sleep. When you wake up, launch the Sleep application to see how much sleep you've had and your sleep trends over the last 14 days.

If your watch is charged below 30% before bedtime, you'll be told to charge it.

You can setup many schedules, for instance, one for days of the week and one on the weekends. You every schedule you can setup the following:

- Sleep goals (how long you want to sleep)
- When you want to go to bed & wake up
- Alarm sound to wake you
- When to activate sleep mode, which would limit distraction before going to bed and it would protect your sleep when you are in bed
- Sleep tracking, which makes use of your gestures to detect sleep when you wear your watch to bed.

Tip: If you want to leave sleep mode, first rotate your watch's Digital Crown. Then open the Controls Centre and tap on the Sleep button .

Setup Sleep on your watch

- Enter the Sleep application on your watch.
- Adhere to the directives on your display.

You can also launch the Health application on your Phone, click the Browse tab, touch Sleep, and click on the Get Started button in the Setup Sleep segment.

Turn off or edit your next wakeup alarm

- Launch the Sleep application on your watch.
- Touch your present bedtime.
- To choose a new wake time, click the wake time, rotate the Digital Crown to choose a new time, and then click on the Check button ✓.
  If you do not want to be waked by your watch, deactivate the alarm.

The change only applies to your next wakeup alarm, after which your normal routine will continue.

Add or change a sleep schedule

- Launch the sleep application on your watch
- Touch Full Schedule, then do any of the below:

- ➢ Adjust your sleeping mode: Click on **Current schedule**.
- ➢ Add a sleeping schedule: Click on Add schedule.
- ➢ Change your sleeping goal: Click on Sleep Goal and then set your sleep duration.
- ➢ Make changes to the wind-down time: Touch Wind Down, and choose when you want sleep mode to be activated before you sleep.
- ❖ Do any of the below:
  - ➢ Choose your schedule days: Click on your schedule, then click the area under Active On. Pick days, and touch Done.
  - ➢ Change your wake & bed time: Click on Wakeup or Bed Time, rotate the Digital Crown to set a new time, and click on Set.
  - ➢ Set the alarm options: activate or deactivate Alarm and touch Sound to select an alarm sound.
  - ➢ Cancel or remove a sleep schedule: Click Delete Schedule (at the lower part of your display) to delete an old schedule, or click Cancel (at the upper part of your display) to cancel the one you are creating.

Adjust sleep options

- Launch the Settings application on your watch.
- Click on Sleep, then touch Sleep Focus to make changes to the following settings:
  - Activate at Wind Down: As a rule, Sleep Focus starts at the wind-down time you choose in the Sleep application. If you want to control Sleep Focus manually in the Controls Centre, disable this option.
  - Sleep Screen: your watch screen and the lock screen of your Phone are simplified to limit distraction.
  - Show Time: Display the time & date on your Phone & watch when sleep mode is active.
- Enable or disable Charging Reminders & sleep Tracking.

  When sleep Tracking is active, your watch would track your sleep and add sleep information to the Health application on your Phone.

  When Charging Reminder is active, your watch would remind you to charge it before your bed-time.

You can also adjust these sleep settings on your Phone. Launch the Health application on your Phone, touch Browse, then head over to Sleep> Options.

Check out your recent sleep history

❖ Launch the sleep application on your watch.
❖ Go down to see how much sleep you had the night before and your average sleep over the last fourteen days.

To view your sleep history on your Phone, enter the Health application on your Phone, click the **Browse** button, and then click on the **Sleep** button.

Check your breathing rate

Your watch can monitor your respiratory rate while you sleep, which can give you a better understanding of your overall health. After putting on your watch to sleep, adhere to the directives below:

❖ Launch the Health application on your Phone, click the **Browse** button, and click on **Respiratory**.
❖ Touch **Respiratory Rate**, and touch Show More Respiratory Rata Data.

VOICE MEMOS APP

Utilize the Voice Memos application ⊕ on your watch to record your notes.

Record a voice memo

❖ Launch the Voice Memo application on your watch.
❖ Click the Recording button ●.
❖ To end a session, touch the end button ■.

Play a voice memo

❖ Launch the Voice Memo application on your watch.
❖ Touch a recording on the Voice Memo screen and touch the Play button ▶ to play it.
❖ To delete the record, press the More button ••• and click the Delete button.

The audio memos you record on your Watch are automatically synchronized to any iOS device, iPad, & Mac that is logged in with the same Apple ID.

WALKIE-TALKIE

Walkie-Talkie is an interesting and easy way to keep in touch with other Apple Watch users. Just like making use of a real walkie-talkie, press a button to talk and release the button to hear what the other person has to say. To use walkie-talkie the two participants need to have connectivity via Bluetooth connection to their iPhone, cellular, or Wi-Fi.

Add your friends to the Walkie-Talkie application

❖ Enter the Walkie-Talkie application on your watch.

❖ Click the Add Friends button, then select a Contact.

❖ Wait for your friend to accept the invitation. The contact card of your friend would remain gray and would appear under your Invited Friends till you're your friend accepts your request. Once they've accepted, the contact card would turn yellow and you and your friend can talk right away.

To remove friends, enter the Walkie-Talkie application, swipe to the left on your friend, and click the Remove icon ✕. Alternatively, launch the Watch application on your Phone, touch Walkie-Talkie> Edit, click on the minus icon ⊖, and then click the Remove button.

How to accept Walkie-Talkie invitations

Touch Always Allow in a message that shows when somebody sends you an invitation. If you do not see the message, you can find it in the Notification Centre and the Walkie-Talkie application.

Start a Walkie-Talkie conversation

- ❖ Enter the Walkie-Talkie application.
- ❖ Click on a Friend.
- ❖ Press the talk key, and say what you want. If "connecting" is displayed on your screen, wait for it to connect. After it has connected, your friend would hear your voice and can reply right away.

As long as your friend is putting on his/her watch and Walkie-Talkie is enabled, they would get alerts whenever you want to speak.

Talk over Walkie-Talkie

- ❖ Hold down the talk key, then say what you want.
- ❖ When you are done, release it. Your friends will hear what you have to say right away.
  Rotate the Digital Crown to adjust the volume.

Activate or deactivate Walkie Talkie

❖ Enter the Walkie-Talkie application.
❖ Activate or deactivate Walkie-Talkie. If somebody wants to contact you when you are not available, a message will appear asking you if you want to talk.

You can also activate or deactivate Walkie Talkie by touching the Walkie-Talkie button in the Controls Centre.

If Silent mode is activated in the Controls Centre, you would only be able to hear chimes & the voice of your friend.

If you cannot find the Walkie-Talkie application

1. FaceTime is needed for Walkie-Talkie to function, so if you have uninstalled the FaceTime application, reinstall it on your iPhone.
2. Ensure FaceTime is activated. Enter the settings application, click on FaceTime and activate FaceTime.
3. Launch the FaceTime application. To ensure that you have setup the FaceTime application correctly, try to make a call.
4. Restart your Watch.
5. Restart your Phone.

APPLE PAY

Apple Pay provides a private, reliable, & easy way to pay for things on your watch.

Add a card to your watch

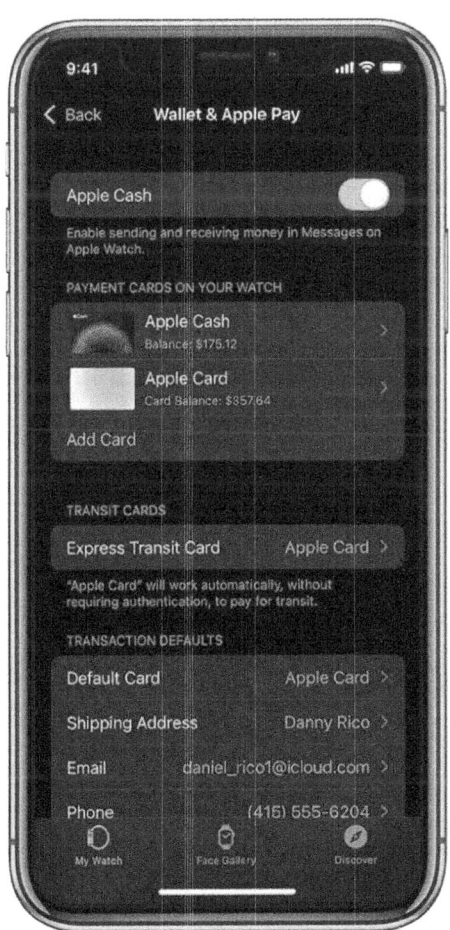

- Enter the Watch application on your Phone.
- Click on My Watch and click on Wallet and Apple Pay.
- If you have a card on another Apple device or have a card you removed recently, click the Add button beside the card you want to add and enter the CVV of the card.
- For other cards, click the Add Card button and adhere to the directives on your screen.

Pick your default card

- Launch the Watch application on your Phone.
- Click on My Watch, Touch Wallet, and Apple Pay, click on Default Card, and choose a card.

Change a card's order

Enter the Wallet application on your watch, long-press a card, then move it to another new position by dragging it there.

Remove a card

- ❖ Enter the Wallet application on your watch.
- ❖ Touch a card to select it.
- ❖ Go down and click the Delete button.

You can also remove a card from your phone, simply enter the Watch application on your Phone, click on **My Watch**, click on Wallet and Apple Pay, click on the card, and click the **Remove Card** button.

Find a card's Device Account Number

After paying for something with your watch, the card's Device Account Number is sent to the seller. To look for the last 4 digits of this number, adhere to the directives below:

- ❖ Enter the Wallet application on your watch.
- ❖ Touch to choose a card and click on Card Information.

Note: After selecting a card you would have to enter your watch's password before you can see the details of the cards.

You can also launch the Watch application on your Phone, touch My Watch, click on Wallet and Apple Pay and click on the Card.

Change your transaction details

You can make changes to your in-application transaction details, which include your phone number, e-mail. Shipping address, & default card.

- Enter the Watch application on your Phone.
- Click on **My Watch**, click on Wallet and Apple Pay and scroll down to see the details.
- Click on an item to change it.

If the Apple Watch is lost or stolen

If your watch is stolen or lost, you can:

- Log in to **appleid.apple.com** with your Apple ID & remove the ability to make payments with your cards in Wallet.
  In the Devices field, select the device and tap on the **Remove All** button in the Apple Pay segment.
  Call your card provider.

Pay for purchase in a store

- Click the Side button two times.

❖ Scroll to pick a card.
❖ Place the watch within a few cm of the contactless card reader and ensure that the screen of your watch faces the reader.

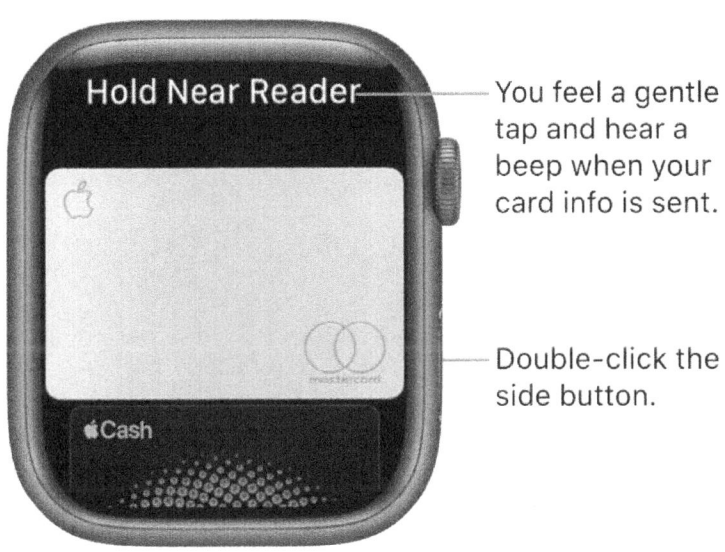

You would feel a soft tap and hear a sound when your payment info is sent. You would get a notification after the transaction has been confirmed.

Buy things in an application

- ❖ When you are buying things in an application with your Watch, select the Apple Pay option when checking out
- ❖ Go through your billing info, shipping, & payment, then click the side button two times to pay with your watch.

Made in the USA
Monee, IL
10 June 2022